Crafts For
an
Old-Fashioned
Christmas

Crafts For an Old-Fashioned Christmas

Edited by Diana Wenk

NELSON DOUBLEDAY, INC.
GARDEN CITY, N. Y.

Acknowledgments

Grateful acknowledgment is made to the following for permission to use their copyrighted material:

"Pill Boxes," "Flower Frame," from *Million Dollar Projects from the 5 & 10¢ Store* by Leslie Linsley, design and photography by Jon Aron. Copyright © 1982 by Leslie Linsley and Jon Aron. Reprinted by permission of St. Martin's Press, Inc.

"Jumping Jack Doll" reproduced from *Christmas Decorations from Williamsburg's Folk Art Collection,* published and copyrighted © 1976 by the Colonial Williamsburg Foundation; distributed by Holt, Rinehart, & Winston.

"Pine Cone Wreath" text, drawings, and photos reproduced from *The Make-It-Merry Christmas Book* by Jeanne Lamb O'Neill. Copyright © 1977 by Jeanne Lamb O'Neill. By permission of William Morrow & Company.

"Straw Angel" from *Christmas Angels* by Phyllis Meras and Julianna Turkevich. Copyright © 1979 by Phyllis Meras and Julianna Turkevich. Reprinted by permission of Houghton Mifflin Company. Drawing reproduced from photo by Alison Shaw.

"Popcorn Tree," "Sugar Cookies," "Fondant Frosting," "Gingerbread Cookies," "Quick Miniature Fruitcakes," "Panettone," "Stollen," "Christmas Twist," "Sweet Dough," "Old-Fashioned Plum Pudding," "Hard Sauce," "Brandy Sauce," "Pilgrim Pie,"

Contents

Introduction

The child wonders at the Christmas Tree:
Let him continue in the spirit of wonder.

T. S. ELIOT

To children, the Christmas Tree is indeed a thing of wondrous beauty that offers gifts of light and life. In the dead of winter, a cheerful wisdom shines forth: The darkness of the world can be overcome. We *can* know love and sense the miraculous all at once.

Christmas memories are filled with simple delights—wrapping presents in golden foil, trimming the tree with silvery ornaments and tinsel, hanging limp and empty stockings on Christmas eve and finding them on Christmas morning—miraculously plump and full of undreamed surprises.

The charm and innocence of an old-fashioned Christmas brings together our own childhood vision of the holiday and our enduring affection for the season. While we may no longer chop down a stately pine or haul in the Yule log, somehow they still exist in our mind as being part of the Christmas spirit. And, while we frantically try to get our shopping done in one day, the idea of making decorations and gifts exists side by side with the sweet sentiment and spiritual significance of the season.

In this fast-paced and stress-filled age, one of the most restorative and beneficial things you can possibly do is to create an atmosphere of old-fashioned warmth with home-made tree ornaments, wreaths, toys, decorations, and cookies and cakes.

The marvelous tree is an appealing, picturesque symbol of Christmas. It is a combination of pagan reverence for woodland spirits and the idea of Christ as the Tree of Life. In medieval Europe, boughs of hawthorn and cherry trees were brought indoors and placed in water so that they could bloom at Christmastime. The domestic tree as we know it today originated in Germany and was brought to England by Queen Victoria in 1841. In fact, what we think of today as "an old-fashioned Christmas" is a nostalgic return to the Victorian Age of Dickens. That magnificent storyteller created a world of goodwill, human kindness, Yuletide cheer and revelry which increases our desire to re-create those wonders of "Christmas past." We long for a time when grievances will be forgotten, suffering will be alleviated, friendships cherished, and families troubled by misunderstanding will be reunited in love.

Along with the Christmas tree and its fragrant and prickly needles, we carry pine boughs and mistletoe across the threshold. Somehow we have a deep need to deck the halls and walls with things from nature, to bring greenery into homes that have become winter-dreary.

When we bring garlands into the house, we again bring in the old idea of woodland spirits, and with mistletoe we bring protection from harm. Mistletoe was also called "all heal." In ancient rituals, the vine was cut up in the woods and distributed to the assembled people. The sprigs were carried home and hung over doorways as a curative and as a protection against evil.

The tradition of bringing in the Yule log was always an occasion for fun and frolic. Oak, pine, ash, and birch were used to warm and light home and hearth throughout the twelve days of Christmas. The lighting of the log was accompanied by music and great revelry . . . and clean hands were a necessary requirement:

Wash your hands, or else the fire
Will not teend to your desire;
Unwashed hands, ye Maidens, know,
Dead the fire, though ye blow.

Ceremonies for Christmas
(c. 1650)

The radiant *warmth* of Christmas shines in the firelight and the Christmas candles. It revives a spirit that has been dulled by a cold and diminishing light. Yes, stopping in the middle of winter to re-create a quintessential warmth that exists within us is indeed an old story.

We welcome snowy days, white Christmases "just like the ones we used to know," ice-skating, and frosty windowpanes . . . all the more because we know the crackling fire and the glowing lights will warm us through and through.

Even if you don't have a fireplace or a Franklin stove, the warmth of an old-fashioned Christmas can be yours. All the wonderful joys of our Christmas heritage can be translated —by you—into creative effort. Baking cookies with your children, making tree ornaments and wreaths, and decorating your house with handmade crafts will bring the true warmth of the season into your home . . . and into your life.

Christmas is a splendid time to develop your capability for love and beauty—and seek out what is wholly human, intimate, and enriching. It is a time to stop in the cold, forbidding winter, and rejoice in the warmth that is newly born.

MERRY CHRISTMAS!

1

Holiday Crafts

Getting Ready

Organizing Your Time

Craftspeople plan their creative time in different ways. Some people seem to organize their lives around Christmas and make craft items all year long. Others gear up a few weeks before Thanksgiving and produce one wonderful tree ornament for everybody on their Christmas list. And there are those who concentrate on three or four gifts that are slowly and carefully handcrafted with love.

Everything in this book is fun, relatively easy to make, and well worth the time and effort you put into it. None of the craft items will put a crimp in your budget. What you will find is a large and varied selection of imaginative projects. Each one is bound to be a success, both in terms of the satisfaction you will get from making a sweet-smelling Della Robbia wreath or a charming Snowflake ornament . . . and the satisfaction that comes from standing back and admiring the results of your own handiwork.

Start by asking yourself: How much time do I want to devote to holiday crafts? Many of the projects (such as Grapevine Wreath, Sachets, and the Swedish Christmas Bird) can be made in one evening and don't require any special knowledge or technique.

1

Look over the projects, then decide on something that tickles your fancy. Gather together the necessary materials and set aside the time. Remember, nothing store-bought can compare with the unique charm of a handmade tree ornament or a handcrafted gift for a special friend.

Thrifty Tips for Scrap Savers

Many of the projects in this book can be made from leftovers in your scrap basket. Felt scraps, yarn, and bits of fabric can all be used. The Snowflake and Swedish Christmas Bird ornaments can be made from scrap paper . . . the grapevine wreath is simply that, a wreath made by twisting grapevines into a circle . . . and there are yarn angels that can be made from leftover yarn.

What you want may be close at hand—like pinecones on your driveway, or honeysuckle in a summer garden (to be used in sachets). Keep a box for usable materials and add to it every now and then. When the holidays arrive, your "odds and ends" box will have a jumbled assortment of just the things you need.

And don't forget the basic Grapevine Wreath. It can be redone every year by intertwining something different into it. Try bittersweet . . . then dried flowers . . . herbs . . . or something inventive from your sewing or knitting basket.

Best Bets for Bazaars

School and church bazaars are held as fund-raisers in most cities and towns at Christmastime. But the task of making the hundreds of craft items usually begins in July. If you want to create multiples of a single item, there are several projects in the book that would work well. Santa Mouse . . . the Straw Angel . . . and Crocheted Mary Jane Christmas Sock are all appealing candidates for a "handmades" booth.

Any one of the wreaths would make a good raffle prize

. . . as would the Knitted Fisherman Christmas Stocking or Christmas Carol Lights. Or you might want to try a box filled with Jumping Jack Dolls or Straw Angels.

A small Christmas tree, set up and decorated with different ornaments, could be the winning prize . . . or Crocheted Christmas Table Tree, along with recipes for stuffed goose and plum pudding.

Handmade items always sell well at bazaars, so make sure there are enough on hand for all the customers.

Gift-Wrapping Ideas

Many of the craft items in this book could be gifts. They can be wrapped in a charming, old-fashioned way. A simple fir sprig placed under the ribbon of a package can make even the most mundane gift paper look more festive. Add a snowy pinecone (wired at the base) and a few fake holly berries and you've got something special.

Here are some other ideas that you can use . . . or that will inspire you to think up your own:

- Wrap all your presents in silver paper and tie with blue satin ribbon. Add a "snowy house" tree ornament to the bow (a wire ornament hanger will hold it securely).

- Try shiny white shelf paper and white lace for a romantic, Victorian look. A bright red heart-shaped gift tag can easily be made out of construction paper or foil.

- Dark, dark green paper and a wide red plaid bow makes a cheerful, traditional gift wrap for a cheerful, traditional man or woman.

- Children love jingle bells or lollipops and candy canes tied to the bow. How about using a jump rope or a

3

sparkly ice-skate lace instead of a ribbon? Or a red bandanna for a teenager?

- You can use wallpaper if the pattern and color are appropriate. Even a kitchen towel with a Christmas motif, or a "calendar" towel can be used to wrap a gift of food.

- For a child's gift card, write out a riddle about what's inside. Then see if he or she can guess.

- Little drawstring bags made out of scraps of Christmas fabric can be used for ornaments or toys.

- Christmas seals or foil snowflakes and stars are always fun to stick all over packages wrapped in red or white tissue paper.

- Use spices as package decorations. Tie little bundles of cinnamon together with a thin gold cord. Add dried flowers or sprigs of dried herbs—sage or tarragon. Shiny chocolate-brown paper makes a nice contrast.

- You can "checkerboard" around a wrapped box with plastic tape, or print NOEL across the top.

- Thick cord or yarn can be used instead of ribbon. Try a *huge* bow on a small present.

- Plain brown wrapping paper can be decorated with all sorts of Christmas messages and drawings. This is one place children of all ages can get in on the act with broad-tipped felt markers and pictures cut from magazines.

Children Can Help

Children are enthusiastic about making ornaments and wreaths. Their little fingers can push and pull the cotton batting for Santa's beard. And they'll also love making Snowflake ornaments out of white paper. And sitting around the kitchen table with the sunlight streaming onto red and green yarn, making scissors and silver foil glint, will evoke pleasant memories of childhood for you.

Some children like doing just one thing—a part of a larger project. And they get better and better at it as they practice. Others like to do a whole project from beginning to end. Be flexible. And set aside enough time so that the cleanup doesn't end in a bad case of the grumps.

Children love wrapping presents—and writing names on gift tags is always a treat. If you give them plain brown or white wrapping paper, they can create their own designs of interplanetary Santas or giant Yule logs burning blue and red flames.

Christmas cards are fun for children to make. Stencils, pictures from magazines, and stickers can all be used with crayons and colored pencils to create imaginative cards. (See Cards for Children to Make.) A child's original drawing is a keepsake for everyone who is lucky enough to receive it . . . but most of all, it's fun to make. And it's a good rainy-day project. Keep a box full of materials on hand for the occasion.

Toys

Today's Santa still has a pack of old-fashioned surprises. Soft, cuddly teddy bears just waiting to be hugged, dollhouses, and gaily painted wooden trains are still the treasured playthings they have always been. A toy that lasts forever in the heart and mind of a child is one that opens the door to her or his imagination. We all remember the fun we had under the Christmas tree with a gingham patchwork horse . . . a doll baby with a complete layette . . . or a smoothly sanded steam engine.

Christmases are filled with memories of toys. Handmade gifts can be wonderfully simple and can last a lifetime. More than the plaything itself, we love the idea that someone has created something beautiful especially for our enjoyment.

To bring some of the enduring pleasure of childhood into this Christmas season, think about giving old-fashioned handmade playthings. Children of all ages delight in fanciful animals and sturdy wooden toys. There's something very satisfying about making a toy. And the result of investing your time and skill may very well be a charming creation . . . evoking squeaks and squeals of happiness that reverberate throughout the house.

The projects you will find in this book are easy to do, and they won't strain your budget. When you're finished, wrap them in brightly colored tissue, put them under the tree or let them peek invitingly from a Christmas stocking. Whichever toy you choose to make will be "best loved" and favorite to the lucky child who receives your gift.

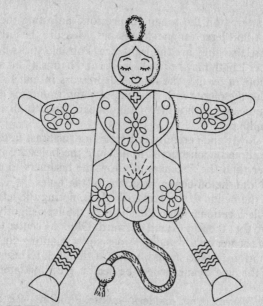

JUMPING JACK DOLL

Contributed by Mrs. Emily Lancaster
Lexington, Virginia

3 wooden tongue depressors
  (6-inch length is best) or 2
  tongue depressors and 2
  Popsicle sticks
Pencil
Ruler
Coping saw
Sandpaper or file
Drill with $\frac{1}{16}$-inch and $\frac{1}{8}$-
  inch bits
Household cement
Paint—yellow, black, red,
  and green
Very fine brush

Medium brush
1-inch wooden bead for
  head, natural color
4 $\frac{1}{2}$-inch brass paper
  fasteners
Pipe cleaner
Carpet thread or other heavy
  thread that will tie
  securely
Tweezers
Metallic string or flat braid
  (for pull string)
Small bead

7

Draw patterns on the tongue depressors, adjusting them if you can't find large tongue depressors. Measure the parts to make sure that they are the right size. Popsicle sticks cut to the proper length may be used for legs and hands. (This saves the trouble of cutting the tongue depressors in half.)

Cut out the pieces with a coping saw and round the edges where indicated with a file or sandpaper. Smooth all edges with sandpaper.

Very slowly and carefully drill holes for the brass fasteners and the thread connections. Make sure the holes are just a bit larger than the fasteners to allow the fasteners to move easily. Note the off-center positions of the holes.

Glue the hands to the arms, tilted up, noting the left and right hole locations. Glue the shoes to the legs slightly off-center so that the feet extend outward. Glue the center to the sides, the center on top and the sides under, slanting outward at the bottom. Space should be left at the back to insert the ends of the pipe cleaner when the head is glued on later. Let dry.

Paint: Sleeves, dress, and legs—white. Pinafore—2 coats of yellow. Head—black hair and features, red mouth. Heads of brass fasteners—yellow. Hands and face—natural wood color. Dress decorations—red flowers, green leaves. Shoes—red. Legs—red and yellow trim.

Double a pipe cleaner to make a loop at the top of the head. Let the ends extend at least 1 inch below the head and glue them at the back in the space between the 2 side pieces.

Run a thread through the smaller drilled holes in the arms and legs. Insert brass fasteners into the large holes of the legs, arms, and body, and turn down the wings of the fasteners with tweezers. Be sure to leave space for free movement of the arms and legs. Tie the threads with a secure knot while the arms and legs are in a downward position. Tie cording onto the arm thread and leg thread in a single knot. Let the cord extend below the doll's shoes by 3 inches. Thread a small bead onto the cording and knot the end of the cord to hold it.

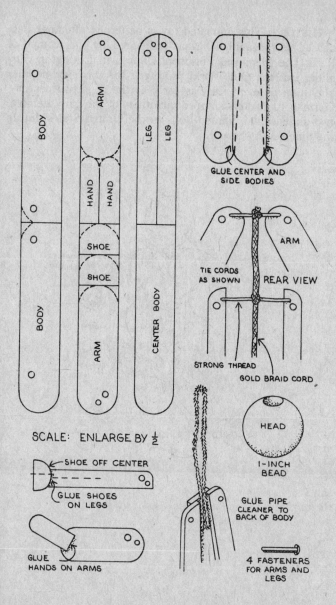

BODY

BODY

ARM

HAND
HAND

SHOE

SHOE

ARM

LEG
LEG

CENTER BODY

GLUE CENTER AND
SIDE BODIES

ARM

REAR VIEW

TIE CORDS
AS SHOWN

STRONG THREAD

GOLD BRAID CORD

SCALE: ENLARGE BY ½

SHOE OFF CENTER

GLUE SHOES
ON LEGS

GLUE
HANDS ON ARMS

HEAD

1-INCH
BEAD

GLUE PIPE
CLEANER TO
BACK OF BODY

4 FASTENERS
FOR ARMS AND
LEGS

HISTORY: This animated toy is patterned after one purchased at the annual bazaar sponsored by the women of R. E. Lee Memorial Episcopal Church in Lexington, Virginia. But the Old World prototype for this ever popular plaything dates at least as early as the sixteenth century. German toymakers shipped quantities of the gaily painted, two-dimensional, jointed dolls to the United States during the nineteenth century.

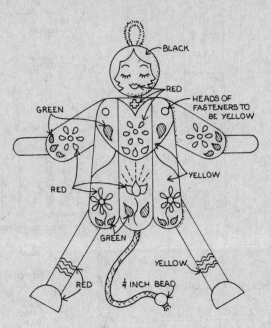

SANTA MOUSE

If you're a collector of Mouseiana, here's the perfect addition. Our crocheted mouse is all dressed for Christmas; in fact, he's making believe he's Santa Claus, complete with his bag of gifts for all the good little mice girls and boys.

Size
Approx 10″ tall

Materials

Worsted weight yarn:

    2 oz gray
    2 oz red
    ½ oz white
    ½ oz gold
    10 yds black
    2 yds green

Size H aluminum crochet hook (or size required for gauge)
3 Gold ¼" jingle bells (for buttons)
Black floral wire: 12" length (for whiskers)
Small felt pieces in black and white
Tracing paper and pencil
White craft glue
Polyester fiber (for stuffing)
Size 16 tapestry needle

NOTE: For whiskers, black carpet thread (stiffened with coating of glue) may be substituted for floral wire.

Gauge

In sc, 7 sts = 2"

Instructions

BODY: Beg at bottom, with gray, ch 2.

Rnd 1: Work 6 sc in 2nd ch from hook. Use small safety pin or piece of yarn in contrasting color and mark last st for end of rnd; move marker at end of each rnd. Do not join rnds.

Rnd 2: Work 2 sc in each sc around = 12 sc.

Rnd 3: * Sc in next sc, 2 sc in next sc; rep from * around = 18 sc.

Rnd 4: Rep Rnd 3 = 27 sc.

Rnd 5: * Sc in each of next 2 sc, 2 sc in next sc; rep from * around = 36 sc.

Rnds 6 through 11: Sc in each sc around.

Rnd 12: * Work 2 sc in next sc, sc in each of next 3 sc; rep from * around = 45 sc.

Rnds 13, 14 and 15: Sc in each sc around. At end of Rnd 15, finish off gray; join red.

Rnds 16 and 17: Continuing with red jacket, sc in each sc around.

Rnd 18: * Sc in each of next 3 sc, dec over next 2 sc. [**To Dec: Draw up a lp in each of next 2 sc, YO and draw through all 3 lps on hook = dec made**]; rep from * around = 36 sc.

Rnds 19 through 23: Sc in each sc around.

Rnd 24: * Sc in each of next 4 sc, dec over next 2 sc; rep from * around = 30 sc. Before working next rnd, stuff body firmly.

Rnd 25: Sc in each sc around.

Rnd 26: * Sc in each of next 3 sc, dec over next 2 sc; rep from * around = 24 sc.

Rnd 27: Sc in each sc around.

Rnd 28: * Sc in each of next 2 sc, dec over next 2 sc; rep from * around = 18 sc.

Rnd 29: Sc in each sc around.

Rnd 30: * Sc in next sc, dec over next 2 sc; rep from * around = 12 sc.

Rnds 31 and 32: Sc in each sc around. At end of Rnd 32, cut yarn, leaving approx 12" sewing length. Finish stuffing body. Set aside, leaving neck open.

JACKET TRIM: With white, ch 45; join with a sl st to form a ring, being careful not to twist chain.

Rnd 1: Ch 1, sc in each ch around; join with a sl st in beg sc = 45 sc.

Rnd 2: Ch 1, sc in same st as joining and in each rem sc around; join with a sl st in beg sc = 45 sc.

Rnd 3: Rep Rnd 2. Finish off; weave in ends. With last rnd worked at top, slip trim over neck and then down around middle of body where colors were changed. Tack in place, if desired.

COLLAR: With white, ch 18, join with a sl st to form a ring. Rep Rnds 1 and 2 of Jacket Trim, having 18 sc in each rnd.

Finish off; weave in ends. With the last rnd worked at bottom, slip collar around neck of body. Tack in place, if desired.

HEAD: Beg at tip of nose, with gray, ch 2.

Rnd 1: Work 4 sc in 2nd ch from hook. As before, mark last of rnd; do not join rnds.
Rnd 2: Work 2 sc in each sc around = 8 sc.
Rnd 3: Sc in each sc around.
Rnd 4: * Sc in next sc, 2 sc in next sc; rep from * around = 12 sc.
Rnds 5 through 8: Rep Rnds 3 and 4, twice. At end of Rnd 6, you should have 18 sc; and at end of Rnd 8, you should have 27 sc.
Rnds 9 through 14: Sc in each sc around.
Rnd 15: * Sc in next sc, dec over next 2 sc; rep from * around = 18 sc.
Rnd 16: Sc in each sc around.
Rnd 17: * Dec over next 2 sc; rep from * around = 9 sc. Cut yarn, leaving approx 8″ sewing length. Stuff head firmly, using pencil to push stuffing down into tip of nose. Thread sewing length into tapestry needle; weave through sts of last rnd. Draw up tightly and fasten securely. Now attach head to body as follows. Thread sewing length left on body (at neck) into tapestry needle. Place head on neck of body, aligning 4th rnd from closure of head at back of neck. Sew in place, having nose protruding over and slightly down over body.

EARS (*make 2*): Beg at bottom edge of outer ear, with gray (leave approx 16″ sewing length), ch 7.

Row 1: Sc in 2nd ch from hook and in each rem ch across = 6 sc.
Row 2: Ch 1, turn; 2 sc in first sc, sc in each of next 4 sc, 2 sc in last sc = 8 sc.
Rows 3 and 4: Ch 1, turn; sc in each sc across.

Row 5: Ch 1, turn; dec over first 2 sc, sc in each sc across to last 2 sc; dec over last 2 sc = 6 sc.

Row 6: Rep Row 5 = 4 sc.

Row 7: Ch 1, turn; (dec over 2 sts) twice = 2 sc. Cut gray, leaving approx 2″ end for weaving in later.

Row 8: With white (for inner ear), ch 1, turn; work 2 sc in each sc = 4 sc.

Row 9: Ch 1, turn; 2 sc in first sc, sc in each of next 2 sc, 2 sc in last sc = 6 sc.

Rows 10, 11 and 12: Rep Rows 3, 4 and 5. At end of Row 12, you should have 4 sc. Finish off; weave in end and 2″ gray end (at end of Row 7). Keeping last row worked to outside of ear, fold piece over at color change. Thread beginning gray sewing length into tapestry needle. Weave bottom and side edges of outer and inner ear tog, cupping ear forward. Position ear on top of head (at back), leaving 3 center sc free between ears; sew in place.

HAT: Beg at cuff, with white, ch 24; join with a sl st to form a ring, being careful not to twist chain. Rep Rnds 1 and 2 of Jacket Trim, having 24 sc in each rnd. Finish off; weave in ends. Turn cuff inside out. With wrong side of sts facing you and foundation chain edge across top, join red with a sl st in unused lp of any st of foundation chain.

Rnd 1: Ch 1, sc in same st as joining and in each rem st around = 24 sc. Mark last st of rnd (as before); do not join rnds.

Rnds 2, 3 and 4: Sc in each sc around.

Rnd 5: * Sc in each of next 4 sc, dec over next 2 sc; rep from * around = 20 sc.

Rnd 6: Sc in each sc around.

Rnd 7: Sc in each of next 3 sc, dec over next 2 sc; rep from * around = 16 sc.

Rnds 8 and 9: Sc in each sc around.

Rnd 10: * Sc in each of next 2 sc, dec over next 2 sc; rep from * around = 12 sc.

Rnds 11, 12 and 13: Sc in each sc around.

Rnd 14: Rep Rnd 10 = 9 sc.

Rnds 15 through 18: Sc in each sc around.

Rnd 19: * Sc in next sc, dec over next 2 sc; rep from * around = 6 sc.

Rnds 20 through 24: Sc in each sc around. At end of Rnd 24, cut yarn leaving approx 6″ end. Thread into tapestry needle; weave through sts of last rnd. Draw up tightly and fasten securely. Make 1″ diameter white pompon (see page 49) and attach to tip of hat. Fold up white cuff. Bend hat as shown in photo and tack into place. Place on head over either ear.

SLEEVE AND MITTEN *(make 2)*: With red (leave approx 12″ sewing length), ch 12; join with a sl st to form a ring.

Rnd 1: Sc in each ch around = 12 sc. Mark last st of rnd (as before); do not join rnds.

Rnds 2 through 5: Sc in each sc around.

Rnd 6: (Dec over next 2 sc) twice, sc in each rem sc around = 10 sc.

Rnds 7, 8 and 9: Sc in each sc around.

Rnd 10: Dec over next 2 sc, sc in each rem sc around = 9 sc.

Rnds 11 and 12: Sc in each sc around.

Rnd 13: Rep Rnd 10 = 8 sc.

Rnd 14: Rep Rnd 10 = 7 sc. Finish off red; join black for mitten.

Rnds 15, 16 and 17: Sc in each sc around. At end of Rnd 17, cut yarn, leaving approx 6″ end. Thread into tapestry needle; weave through sts of last rnd. Draw up tightly and fasten securely. Stuff and shape sleeve and mitten, bending sleeve slightly at elbow. Thread beginning red sewing length into tapestry needle. Sew open edge of sleeve tog, carefully matching 6 corresponding sc across. Then sew this edge to side of mouse in second rnd below white collar.

SLEEVE CUFF *(make 2)*: With white, ch 8, join with a sl st to form a ring. Rep Rnds 1 and 2 of Jacket Trim, having

16

8 sc in each rnd. Finish off; weave in ends. With last rnd worked at top, slip cuff over mitten and position around end of sleeve where colors were changed. Tack in place, if desired.

TAIL: With gray, make a chain to measure approx 14″ long; then work sl st in 2nd ch from hook and in each rem ch across. Cut yarn, leaving approx 4″ sewing length. Thread into tapestry needle and sew tail to body at lower center of back.

Bow: With green, make a chain to measure approx 12″ long; finish off. Knot and trim each end of chain. Tie chain into a bow around tail, approx 1″ from end.

SANTA'S PACK: With gold, work same as Body through Rnd 11.

Rnds 12 through 16: Sc in each sc around.
Rnd 17 (beading rnd): Sl st in next sc, ch 3; dc in each rem sc around, join with a sl st in top of beg ch-3.
Rnd 18: Ch 1, sc in same st as joining and in each rem st around; join with a sl st in beg sc.
Rnd 19: Rep Rnd 18. Finish off; weave in ends.

Drawstring: With black, make a chain to measure approx 15″ long; finish off. Weave through sts of Beading Rnd, beg and ending at beg of rnd. Knot both ends of drawstring tog; trim ends. Place Christmas candy or small toy inside of pack; pull drawstring slightly closed and place over either arm.

FINISHING

Buttons: With sewing thread, attach 3 jingle bells evenly spaced down front center of jacket.
Nose: With gray, make ¼″ diameter pompon and attach to head at tip of nose.
Eyes: Trace outlines on paper. Cut outlines and use as patterns on felt as indicated. With glue, attach felt pieces as shown in photo.

eyes: (2 layers)
glue black on white

Whiskers: Cut floral wire into 3 equal lengths (each approx 4" long). Refer to photo for position and pull each length through end of nose with crochet hook. Dab the ends of each wire with glue to prevent fraying.

Ornaments

A Christmas tree is "old-fashioned." It's hard to imagine trimming a tree with tinsel, lights, colored balls, and little Santas, and having it look like anything else but the Victorian tree that is imprinted in our minds. While visions of sugarplums may no longer dance in our heads, the image of the tree all decorated is still there.

Whether we buy our tree in a shopping mall or go into damp woods and chop down a well-shaped pine, we all think of the tree as a glorious Christmas symbol. Its fresh, clear fragrance and sticky boughs always bring back strong memories—and a resolve to make *this* Christmas the best ever. Again we've come to decorate what was, a few moments ago, just "ordinary." The ornaments shine; we see ourselves smiling in the golden luster. And then the tinsel . . . and the lights twinkling on and off. We've succeeded in making the ordinary into something extraordinary, a magical winking, blinking spectacle which—as we look at it—certainly is the best.

Making Christmas ornaments is very much part of Christmas tradition. Schoolchildren bring home paper balls scribbled and scrawled with red crayon. And grandmothers fashion lacy angels with white-sequined halos. If we're lucky, we buy red velvet ornaments at church bazaars . . . or find a box of crocheted Santas and reindeer in a thrift shop.

Look over last year's ornaments. Then decide what ornament would give the tree more old-fashioned charm. White paper Snowflakes? Straw Angels? Swedish Christmas Birds?

Take your pick. All the projects have been selected with you in mind. The step-by-step instructions will give you the necessary expertise—and the designs you create will look great on your tree whether it's short and bushy or tall and stately.

This year make your own hand-crafted ornaments for your tree—and for gifts. There's nothing more rewarding than packing and wrapping a handmade ornament in crinkling tissue and bringing it as a gift to a tree-trimming party. Or you may decide to have your own tree-trimming party. Ask everyone to bring materials, and then have the fun of making the ornaments together. After you've trimmed the tree, bring out the Christmas cookies and cakes.

PAPER SNOWFLAKE

Snowflakes are particularly appealing when they are hung in clusters from a hallway ceiling or in the archway between

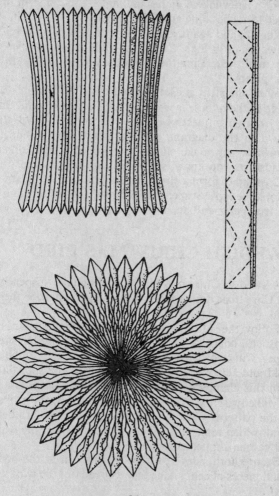

living room and dining room. Make them of white tissue paper.

Start with a Strip

For a snowflake 6 inches in diameter, cut a strip of tissue paper 18 inches long and 6 inches wide. Fold in half, then in half again, and again, and so on until your strip is folded up to a width of ½ inch. Crease the folds carefully, open up the strip, and then, using the creases as a guide, refold in accordion pleats.

When the strip is again folded up to a width of ½ inch, staple in the middle, across the width. (See sketch.) Snip out tiny triangular pieces on each side of the folded strip, as shown in the diagram, and cut points on the ends. Each snowflake you make should be snipped a little differently, because, as you know, snowflakes are never alike.

Open up to form a circle and fasten the sides together with cellophane tape. Suspend by a thread slipped through one of the triangular cutouts.

SWEDISH CHRISTMAS BIRD

The Swedish Christmas bird is traditionally suspended over the Christmas dinner table, bringing good luck to the household.

Follow the pattern given here. The body of the bird is made of Bristol board or cardboard. The wings and tail are tissue paper. Cut two strips, each 5 inches wide and 9 inches long. Fold and snip the strips exactly as with the snowflake that is in this chapter.

Make two slits in the body, as indicated by the broken lines in the pattern. With manicure scissors (or embroidery scissors), widen each slit to about $\frac{1}{16}$ inch so that the wings and tail can be slipped through.

Secure both sides of the wings and tail to the body with small pieces of cellophane tape. Spread out the wings. Fasten

22

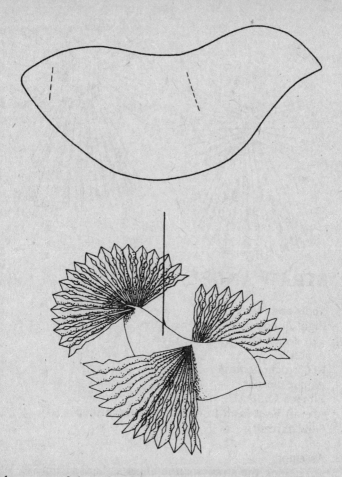

the center of the tail together with cellophane tape so that it forms a semicircle. Suspend the bird by a thread run through the body at a point off-center toward the back, making sure the bird is properly balanced. You may have to experiment to find the balance point.

The birds are made in all colors and in white.

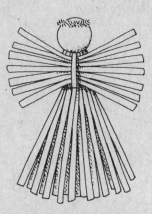
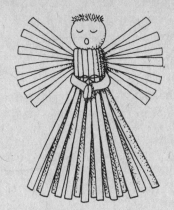

STRAW ANGEL

Tools and materials
Eight 3-inch straws for the wings
Ten 6-inch straws for the dress
A needle
Red crochet cotton
A pipe cleaner
Elmer's Glue-All
A craft bead head from a crafts-supply shop
Gold thread

Assembly
   1. Pick the straw for the angel at harvest time in late summer or early fall, preferably before there is much rain, for it will turn straw brown.
   2. Soak the straw for four hours in warm water.
   3. Clean the straw by cutting away the outer joints and removing the outer casing. From each straw, you should get three straws of different lengths.

24

4. Mark each of the wing straws in the center with a pencil. Push a fine needle through them at the pencil mark.

5. Wind crochet cotton around the straws twice close under the needle and pull the thread tight. The straws will expand into a flat double fan. Tie a firm double knot. Snip the thread, leaving ¼ of an inch. Remove the needle.

6. Take the ten dress straws and gather them into a bunch 3 inches in diameter. Tie them tightly in the middle with red thread and they will flare slightly.

7. Straw by straw, bend the upper section of these dress straws down over the lower section *(as in Drawing),* turning

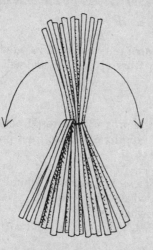

the bundle as you work, thus covering all the thread. If you hold all these straws tightly together there will be a resultant hole in the middle of the bundle.

8. Cut off a pipe cleaner to about 2 inches in length. Dip its end into Elmer's glue and insert it into the craft bead, creating a head and neck. Insert this head and neck into the hole in the center of the straws.

9. Now lift up one of the straws at the back of the head and place the wings under that straw. Draw the straw back into place and tie the bodice ½ inch below the neck with the red thread. Tie it very tightly so the skirt flares as much as possible.

10. Use the lowest of the wing straws for the arms. Bend them forward to make elbows and tie the wrists close together near the body with the red thread. Turn the ends to make tiny hands clasped in prayer.

11. Tie fine gold thread around the angel's neck to hang it from the tree.

CROCHETED SNOWFLAKES

designed by Mary Thomas

Lacy snowflakes are pretty to hang in a window, a doorway, or on a tree. They work up quickly, and will make treasured gifts.

Sizes
Snowflake No. 1, approx 3½″ across from side to side.
Snowflake No. 2, approx 6″ across from point to point.

Materials
Bedspread-weight crochet cotton in white:
    12 yds for Snowflake No. 1, or
    20 yds for Snowflake No. 2
Size 5 steel crochet hook *(or size required for gauge)*

Gauge
In dc, 8 sts = 1″

SNOWFLAKE NO. 1

Instructions
Ch 8, join with a sl st to form a ring.

Rnd 1: Ch 4, work 23 trc in ring, join with a sl st in top of beg ch-4.

snowflake 2

snowflake 1

Rnd 2: Ch 3, do not turn; dc in same st as joining, * † ch 6, sl st in 5th ch from hook (for picot) †; rep from † to † twice (3 picots now made), ch 1, sk next 3 trc, work 2 dc in next trc; rep from * 4 times more, then rep from † to † 3 times (for last picot lp); ch 1, sk last 3 trc, join with a sl st in top of beg ch-3 = 6 picot lps.

Rnd 3: Ch 4, do not turn; trc in next dc, * † ch 6, sl st in 5th ch from hook (for picot) †; rep from † to † 4 times (5 picots now made), ch 1, trc in each of next 2 dc (between picot lps); rep from * 4 times more, then rep from † to † 5 times; ch 1, join with a sl st in top of beg ch-4. **Do not finish off;** continue with same thread and work hanger.

HANGER: Ch 20, do not turn; sl st in next trc, finish off. Weave in ends securely.

Finishing
Wash, block and starch.

27

SNOWFLAKE NO. 2

Instructions

Ch 6, join with a sl st to form a ring.

Rnd 1: Ch 1, work 12 sc in ring, join with a sl st in beg sc.

Rnd 2: Do not turn; * ch 16, sl st in next sc; rep from * 10 times more, ch 7, work a triple trc in sl st (st used to join prev rnd). **[To work triple trc: (YO hook) 4 times, insert hook in sl st and draw up a lp (6 lps now on hook), work (YO hook and draw through 2 lps on hook) 5 times = triple trc made]** = 12 lps. *(NOTE: Last lp was formed by working ch 7 and triple trc, and brings thread into position to beg next rnd.)*

Rnd 3: Do not turn; * ch 6, sc over center of next lp; rep from * 10 times more, ch 3, sk ch-7 of last lp, dc in top of triple trc of same lp = 12 lps. *(NOTE: Last lp was formed by working ch 3 and dc, and brings thread into position to beg next rnd.)*

Rnd 4: Ch 6, do not turn; work 3 dc in first lp (over last dc of prev rnd), * work (3 dc, ch 3, 3 dc) in next lp; rep from * 10 times more, work 2 dc in first lp (next to ch-6 and first 3 dc of rnd), join with a sl st in 3rd ch of beg ch-6.

Rnd 5: Do not turn; sl st into next ch-3 sp, ch 5, work a double trc in same sp. **[To work double trc: (YO hook) 3 times, insert hook in sp and draw up a lp (5 lps now on hook), work (YO hook and draw through 2 lps on hook) 4 times = double trc made]** * Ch 5, 2 double trc in same sp; ch 11 (for lp at point), 2 double trc in same sp; ch 5, 2 double trc in same sp; ch 5, sk next two 3-dc groups, sc in next ch-3 sp; ch 5, sk next two 3-dc groups, 2 double trc in next ch-3 sp; rep from * around, ending last rep without working last 2 double trc, join with a sl st in top of beg ch-5. Finish off and weave in ends.

Finishing

Starch and block snowflake same as for Snowflake No. 1. For hanger, use a piece of white or translucent nylon thread (or fishing line) to tie a loop at one point of snowflake.

Wreaths

What would Christmas be without a wreath on the front door or in the living-room window? Your family and friends will take joyful note of it. Even bluejays at the bird-feeder and bushy-tailed squirrels seem to notice that something is different. Christmas is afoot, creeping ahead as slowly as deer making their way through snowy woods.

Wreaths look at home almost anywhere: over the mantel, in a foyer, at the top of the stairs. A punch bowl filled with foamy eggnog looks more elegant and festive if you place it inside a pine wreath that has been set on the table. Trim the wreath with tiny ornaments or little silver balls and a wide red velvet ribbon.

Making a wreath is much more fun than just going out and buying one. It's easy and very special. Once you start, it's hard to stop. Soon you'll be making one for every window in the house . . . and giving them as gifts.

A grapevine wreath is a sophisticated and popular version. Once you get the "vine" part made, the possibilities for decorating it are almost endless. Try combinations of dried flowers . . . or just bittersweet.. Plaid ribbons are cheery. Practically anything you can think of will probably look good. Here's a chance to be really inventive. If you find yellow ribbon in your scrapbox, try it. Add a few sprigs of dried yellow and purple statice and you've got something really original. If you prefer a wreath that's more traditional, intertwine holly or mistletoe in the grapevine. Try making a 6-inch wreath for your kitchen. It will give you a lift early in the morning when you're enjoying your first cup of coffee, or when you're faced with cleaning up after Christmas dinner.

Wreaths can be pine circles or a wonderful roundness created out of seeds and pods and nuts. A wreath can be a red and green needlework piece that has been stuffed and plumped like a pillow. Whatever the material, the shape remains the same. An O, as cheerful and vibrant as the beginning of a Christmas carol: "O, come all ye faithful . . ."

Pick out the wreath that strikes your fancy. The designs have been chosen with you in mind. We wanted to give you a varied and interesting selection so that you can use your knowledge and ability to create a beautiful decoration for your home. Making a wreath is an old-fashioned pleasure that has never gone out of style. Enjoy the work. And enjoy the product of the work. When the Christmas wreath is in the window, you can admire it all the more because it reflects your special talent.

SEED-POD WREATH

For a change from the usual evergreen wreath, one made of dried plant materials is colorful and interesting. Many different kinds of materials can be used: rose hips, acorn caps, teasel pods, astilbe blossoms, snowberries (some will dry white, some dark), coneflower pods, burdock, day-lily pods, and beechnut pods. The assortment gives the wreath its charm.

As a base you can use a Styrofoam circle of whatever size you like. Or you can cut a circle of heavy cardboard or corrugated cardboard as a base. If you cover the base carefully and completely, the edges of the base will not show.

Attach the seed pods with white glue (Sobo or Elmer's), and mix the assortment as you go. The variation of color and texture, shape and form, will create an unusual wreath. To preserve it, spray with a clear plastic.

Tie a red ribbon on the wreath, or leave it completely plain. Either way, it will decorate your doorway beautifully.

31

DELLA ROBBIA WREATH

Skill Level
Elementary.

Materials
Dried grasses, natural color and/or desired dyed color, 5–7" lengths
Plastic lemons and/or other fruit, no larger than 1" diameter
Silk flowers and leaves
Satin ribbon: ⅛" wide, 6" length; ½" wide, ⅔ yard
Lightweight wire

Directions
Arrange bunches of grasses into a 5½"-diameter circle, interspersing dyed colored grasses with natural grasses if desired; wire grasses where necessary to hold all pieces in place and to maintain circular shape. Add silk flowers and leaves all around wreath; wire in place securely, making sure wires are hidden. Wire lemons and/or other fruit around wreath. Tie ⅛" ribbon into a small bow; wire to wreath near section that will be top. Cut 12" length of ½" ribbon; tie into a bow and wire to wreath near bottom. Fold remaining ribbon in half; tie or sew ends together to form a hanging loop. Wire loop to top of wreath.

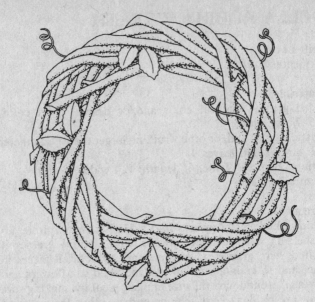

GRAPEVINE WREATH

Early fall is a good time to gather wild grapevines for wreaths. They're more flexible at this time and easier to work with. You can find grapevines growing in the woods and at roadsides. Clip the vines carefully, along with the spidery tendrils that are attached and grow every which way. You'll need about eight vines; each one should be about six feet long. Strip the leaves off the vine and form a circle eighteen inches in diameter. As you go around again, twist the vine and weave it into the circle. Tuck the end in and continue twisting the remaining vines into the wreath.

You can experiment with sizes and textures. A large woody wreath is handsome on the front door, while a delicate smaller version with fine-textured vines would look attractive in an entryway . . . at the top of a staircase . . . or on the dining room door.

After you have finished making the wreath, lay it flat and place it in a warm, dry place for about two weeks, or until the green vines turn brown. You can decorate the wreath with straw flowers, bittersweet, baby's breath, or dried peppers . . . or you can intertwine gingham ribbon or green velvet ribbon, and then tie a bow.

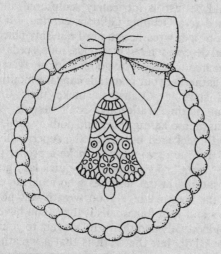

CRANBERRY WREATH

For an inside door, you can make a colorful wreath by stringing cranberries on a wire, bending the wire into a circle and attaching another wire to hang it by.

Tie a red or green velvet ribbon bow to the wreath at the point where the wires meet, and hang an angel or a Santa Claus or a bell—or any one of your special Christmas treasures—inside the wreath.

The cranberries should be lacquered (clear nail polish will do nicely) in order to preserve them for the entire holiday season.

35

PINE CONE WREATHS

The trouble with most pinecone wreaths that you see for sale is that they contain pinecones—period. They'd make Grinling Gibbons turn over in his Westminster Abbey grave. Gibbons was the seventeenth-century master woodcarver who was Sir Christopher Wren's pet, and a *proper* pinecone wreath should be just as intricately sculptured and elaborately designed as a Grinling Gibbons carving.

To make a proper wreath, you need not only pinecones of every size and description but also pods, nuts, seeds, and pits —at least one hundred separate goodies for an average-sized wreath. Just gathering your materials can take months. (Garden-clubbers start in August to make their Christmas wreaths.) But, if time's afleeting, don't despair. You can order all kinds of fascinating cones and pods by mail, and you can cheat with packaged nuts from the supermarket.

Basically, there are two ways to make a proper pinecone wreath—the "right" way and the jiffy-quick lazy girl's way. For years I sneered at the slouches who took the easy way out; to me, the measure of a good wreath was how many tedious hours and torn fingernails it took (you have to wire each piece individually and then wire it again to your frame). I hate to backslide, but the truth is that a wreath slapped together with linoleum paste looks *almost* as good to me, and probably just as gorgeous to everybody else. Your masterpiece may not endure unto eternity, but it will last long enough to suit most people. You'll find directions for both methods here (but do resolve to take the hard path of virtue *next* year).

MATERIALS FOR WIRED WREATH
Tree cones of all kinds (pine, hemlock, cedar, larch, piñon, spruce, redwood, sequoia, cypress, etc.)
Other materials (sweet gum balls, horse chestnuts, acorns,

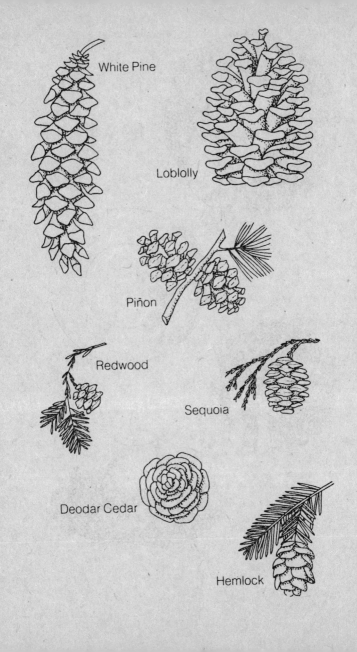

nuts of all kinds, peach pits, prune seeds, cotton pods, eucalyptus pods, beech pods, etc.)

Pegboard ring, cut to size at lumber yard (wreaths shown measure 14 inches at outer diameter, 7 inches at inner diameter)

Wire cutters

Electric drill

Florists' wire, #22 or #24

Clear plastic spray

Pliers

OPTIONAL

Artificial lady apples or other fruit

Baby's breath or other dried flowers

Velvet ribbon

Gold spray

Cotton felt, for backing

DIRECTIONS

Gather materials. The best time to collect fallen cones and pods is in the early fall before they become dark, weathered, or damaged. For hard-to-find specimens such as deodar roses, piñon cones, and eucalyptus pods, order from mail-order sources.

Rinse dirty cones quickly under hose or faucet spray. To dry cones and open up their scales, place on aluminum foil in a warm (150-degree) oven. Or preheat oven to 250 degrees and then turn off. Length of drying time depends on wetness of cones. Another method of cleaning cones is to soak them overnight in a bucket of water. For prolonged drying, cover with damp newspapers to keep cones from overbrowning.

When cones are dry, slice some into "flowers" with wire cutters. The cut ends will look like single-petaled flowers, the tips like chubbier blossoms.

Nuts and acorns must also be pre-baked to kill any lurking wildlife. Before baking, drill holes for wiring with electric drill.

Cones are easily wired by twisting thin florists' wire between the scales at the base. Wire each piece separately before you start to assemble your wreath. Group small cones, nuts, and acorns into clusters. Also, before you start, drill still more holes into the pegboard ring—remember, you have hundreds of pieces to wire on.

Next, plan your design, starting with the larger whole cones first. You'll find that an outer ring of overlapping look-alike cones, plus an inner ring of smaller cones, works best. (The large wreath shown is ringed with white pinecones on the outside, loblolly cones on the inside.) Keep adding materials and building up your wreath until every last fat, chunky inch is filled.

Use a pair of pliers to tighten your wires. As you go along, new pieces can be wired in back to already fastened wires. When you get to the final pieces, it will help enormously to prop your work on an easel so that light shines through the pegboard holes.

Now it's time to spray. Use several coats of clear plastic to polish and preserve your wreath. Believe me, when you finally behold your masterpiece in all its rich, glossy, mahogany-brown glory, you won't regret a minute of your toil and trouble.

Next come the finishing touches. Tie off and trim with wire cutters the excess wires in back, leaving a sturdy loop for hanging. Glue on a circle of felt to hide the jungle of wires and to protect your wall or door. Add trims—fruits, velvet bows, sprigs of dried flowers—or a *very light* dusting of gold spray. Of course, minus Christmasy frills, your wreath can hang proudly all year long. If you store it, in a tightly sealed plastic bag, be sure to add a handful of mothballs.

MATERIALS FOR EASY LINOLEUM PASTE WREATH

Cones and pods, as for the wired wreath

Ring base (cut from solid plywood at the lumber yard or ordinary corrugated cardboard at home)

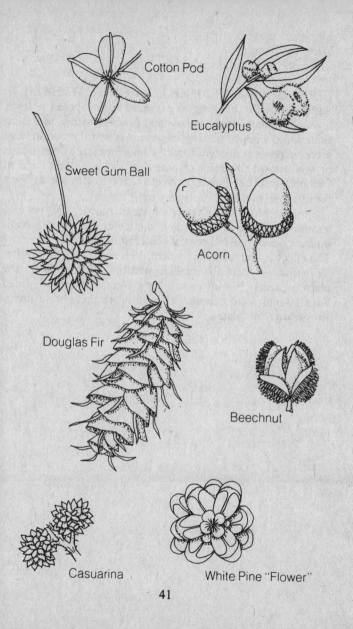

Cotton Pod

Eucalyptus

Sweet Gum Ball

Acorn

Douglas Fir

Beechnut

Casuarina

White Pine "Flower"

41

Linoleum paste
Wire, for hanging
Clear plastic or gold spray

DIRECTIONS FOR LINOLEUM PASTE WREATH

Attach wire for hanging to plywood base. Spread a thick layer of linoleum paste on base and proceed with your design as in wired wreath, placing larger cones first. Dip additional pieces in paste as needed. Luckily, linoleum paste dries a dark brown, almost the color of pinecones, so you don't have to fuss and fret. Set finished wreath aside to dry for at least twenty-four hours before spraying.

Spray with several coats of clear plastic. Or gold. I wouldn't dream of burying a meticulously wired wreath under a heavy-handed coat of gold, but in this case, why not? The effect is marvelously opulent, Victorian, and, to be sure, Christmasy—great for quickie wreaths for friends or the church bazaar. For an even jiffier project, try a small gilded 8- or 10-inch solid plaque. (You can work these on ordinary throwaway pie plates.)

Gifts to Make

The exchange of gifts at Christmastime is a happy ceremony that combines the wonderful sound of unfolding tissue paper with the delightful surprise that is suddenly revealed. A handmade gift is especially charming because it conveys thoughtfulness and an old-fashioned flavor that is missing in today's fast-paced holidays.

Traditionally, a gift can be as extravagant as a silver-fox hat, or as practical as a navy-colored scarf. But no matter how much effort you put into shopping, it isn't the same as making a gift for someone you care about. Handcrafted presents and the spirit of Christmas go hand-in-hand.

The gifts-to-make that you'll find on the following pages range from sachets to Crocheted Ice Skate Decoration. Each one would make a wonderful gift and can be packaged in a unique way. Stack the sachets in a small straw basket, for example.

The section for children includes easy and imaginative presents that they will take delight in making. Wouldn't Grandpa love a Pebble Paperweight? And wouldn't Mom like Animal Clips to hold her recipes?

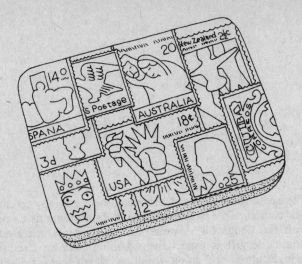

PILL BOXES

Sucrets or candy tins are good sizes to hold pills or vitamins. They fit easily into a purse or pocket and can be decorated in a variety of ways. The elegant boxes shown here were made by J.R. Trzcinski and are an example of how an ordinary item can be designed in a sophisticated way.

The technique is decoupage and the paper cutouts come from wrapping paper, greeting cards, or similar sources. The directions here have been simplified from the traditional decoupage method for quick and easy crafting.

Materials
Sucrets tin
Acrylic paint
Small brush
Clear varnish or nail polish
Paper designs
Cuticle scissors

White glue
Sponge

Directions

Paint the outside of the box, including the hinges and bottom. Let the paint dry, then apply a second coat. The background color used here is royal blue.

Select and cut out paper illustrations that will fit on the lid. Glue each one in place. Pat away excess glue with a damp sponge. For a variation you can use stamps, stars, labels, seals, or heart stickers as designs. Check the school-supply sections for more ideas. Consider covering the lid with rows of white buttons if it is to hold buttons or pins.

Coat the entire box with varnish or nail polish and let dry with the lid propped open slightly. Apply 2 or 3 more coats allowing each to dry between applications.

The inside can be left as is, or painted or lined with paper.

FLOWER FRAME

Frames are expensive. Even plain black metal frames cost a lot, but are the least expensive and they are dependably available for any size picture. The problem is that they aren't very good-looking. A scrap of cotton fabric, some acrylic paint, and tiny artificial flower buds can change that.

Materials

Frame
Piece of cotton fabric
Small tube of red and white acrylic paint
Brush
A stalk of small blue artificial flowers and another of pink
Spray varnish
Scissors
Rubber cement (school or art supplies)
Razor blade

Directions

Remove the glass and cardboard backing from the frame.

Mix a small drop of red into a tablespoon full of white acrylic paint to get a pale pink. Give the frame 2 coats of paint, allowing the first to dry before applying the second.

Cut a piece of fabric the size of the cardboard backing. Coat the back of the fabric and front of the cardboard with rubber cement and let dry.

Carefully place the fabric over the cardboard and smooth down. Measure the photograph to be used. Using the razor blade, cut a square that's slightly smaller in the center of the fabric-covered board.

Touch up the inside edge of the cut square with the pink paint. Tape the photo to the back of the opening.

Cut the buds from the plastic stalks. Arrange them approximately an inch apart and glue them around the frame alternating the colors. Let them dry. Spray the flowered frame with 1 or 2 coats of clear varnish. Reassemble the frame and hang.

SWEET SACHETS

Grandma put lavender sachets into her drawers to give her lingerie a sweet scent. The dried flowers gave off a refreshing fragrance that drove away musty odors.

Dried flowers of all sorts can be used for sachets: carnations, peonies, roses, lilacs, lily-of-the-valley, honeysuckle, and geraniums. You can dry them yourself or purchase potpourri mixtures.

The fun is in making little bags to hold the petals. "Sachet" literally means "little bag" in French. A 3 × 4-inch fabric bag can be trimmed with lace and filled with about ½ cup of the dried flowers, then tied with a velvet ribbon.

Making sachets is a scrapsaver's delight. Remember that beige brocade dress you made last year? Here's your chance to use the leftover fabric. And what about that white tulle you used for Sarah's ballet costume?

Getting a sachet bag as a gift is a real treat, and you'll be remembered every time the drawer is opened and the subtle scent of flowers wafts into the room.

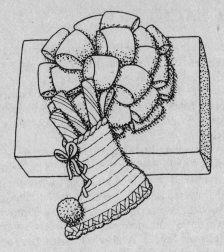

CROCHETED ICE SKATE DECORATION

adapted from a design by Sue Penrod

Size
Approx 1½" wide *(across top)* × 2½" long *(from top edge to bottom of blade)*

Materials
Worsted weight yarn:
   10 yds white
   2½ yds red
   2 yds gray
Size I aluminum crochet hook *(or size required for gauge)*

Gauge
In sc, 7 sts = 2"

Instructions

Beg at top, with white (leave approx 12″ end for working loop later), ch 10, join with a sl st to form a ring. *(NOTE: All rnds are worked on outside of skate.)*

Rnd 1: Sc in each ch around = 10 sc. *NOTE: Do not join; work continuous rnds. Use a small safety pin or piece of yarn in contrasting color and mark first st of rnd; move marker at beg of each rnd.*

Rnds 2 through 4: Sc in each sc around for 3 rnds.

Rnd 5: Sc in next sc, dec over next 2 sc **(To work Dec: Draw up a lp in each next 2 sc, YO hook and draw through all 3 lps on hook = dec made).** Sc in each of next 2 sc, 2 sc in each of next 4 sc, sc in next sc = 13 sc.

Rnd 6: Sc in each of next 6 sc, 2 sc in next sc; work (sc, hdc) in next sc, work (hdc, sc) in next sc; 2 sc in next sc, sc in each of next 3 sc = 17 sts.

Rnd 7: Sc in each of next 9 sc, 2 sc in each of next 2 hdc, sc in each of next 6 sc = 19 sc.

Rnd 8: Sc in each of 19 sc around, sc in next sc (first st of rnd), sl st in next sc. Finish off white.

BLADE: Join gray with sl st in 2nd st of rnd (where last sl st was just worked). Pinch opening closed. **Working through both sides at the same time,** work (hdc, sc) in next st, sc in each of next 7 sts, work (hdc, ch 2, sl st) in last st. Finish off; weave in ends.

LOOP: Insert hook in st at top edge under beg yarn end, hook yarn end and draw through st; ch 10, join with a sl st in same st. Finish off; weave in end securely.

LACE: Thread 18″ strand of red into tapestry or yarn needle. Beg at center top of skate and work 3 cross sts evenly spaced down center front of skate. Tie ends of lace into a bow and trim ends evenly.

POMPON: Make a ½″ diameter red pompon as follows: Wrap yarn around tines of dinner fork; then tie wrapped yarn securely between the center of the tines. Cut looped ends and

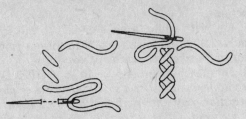

trim to ½ ″ diameter size. Attach pompon securely to toe end of skate.

GIFTS FOR CHILDREN TO MAKE

LUGGAGE SPOTTERS

Here's the perfect gift for people who travel a lot. Yarn pompons wired to suitcases are easy to find at airports. For a generous gift, pack three pompons in a plastic sandwich bag.

To Make Spotters: Bend one side of a coat hanger to make a yarn-winder 2½ ″ wide. Wind with 2 colors of yarn, a total of 50 times around. Use a bit of masking tape to hold yarn ends while you tie pompon with wire. With wire cutters, cut 2 pieces of thin wire 10″ long and twist them around middle of yarn—use pliers to twist tight. Cut yarn loops next to coat hanger to make pompon.

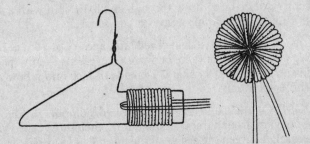

PEBBLE PAPERWEIGHT

Look for flat smooth stones about 1–1½″ long. If they're dark, paint them white; then paint on bright green Christmas trees.

- Glue decorated stones to inside of a large jar lid to make a paperweight. Glue a felt circle on bottom of paperweight. (This will cover printing on jar lid.)

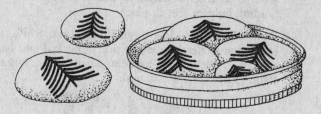

SPRUCE TREE CONE BIRDS

Scales on spruce tree cones are softer and curlier than scales on pine cones—they'll look like feathers when you snip them into bird shapes.

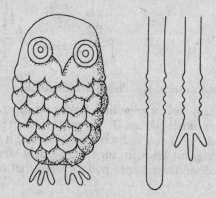

- Base of cone is top of bird's head. Mark 1 scale near top to be bird's beak; then, with scissors, snip off scales around beak to shape head and neck of bird. Cut beak scale to a point.

- To make base for feet, so bird will stand, cut off tip of cone opposite head. Stuff bits of tissue in between cut scales to make base flat.

- Bend hairpins to look like bird's feet (see diagram); glue to base. Glue circle of heavy paper over base holding hairpin feet in place.

- Paint thumbtacks like targets, black and white, for eyes; glue to head on either side of beak. Paint beak orange, or outline it in white so it can be clearly seen. Paint entire bird if you wish.

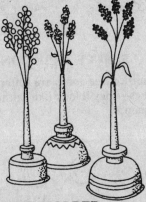

WEED HOLDER

You can make a great little holder for dried flowers or weeds from a small oil can. (If you want to shorten it, have Daddy cut off tip of can with tin snips.) Enamel it any bright color. When paint dries, arrange a few bright strawflowers in it— or a dried flower, seed pod, or weed that has an interesting shape.

FINGERPRINT NOTEPAPER

Decorate plain white notepaper with flowers and birds and animals you make from your own fingerprints.

You'll need: *Stamp pad; felt pen with a fine tip; notepaper*

Press your finger on the stamp pad and then on notepaper. By using fingers and thumb, and by rolling the finger, you can make a variety of shapes and sizes of prints.

- Now use your imagination to decorate the fingerprints. What do they look like? Pussy willows? Butterflies? Kittens? Use the felt pen to add stalks to pussy willows, stems to flowers, tail and ears to cats, or to outline butterfly wings.

- One-color designs are very attractive, but you can print notepaper in more than one color if you have stamp pads and pens in different colors.

FISH PRINT FOR DADDY

You use a real fish to make this work of art.

You'll need: *a whole fresh fish (flat ones work best); hair spray; two 1" brushes; waterproof India ink and rice paper (from art supply store); newspapers; straight pins*

Place fish on a pad of newspapers; fan fins open and pin them down to newspaper padding with straight pins. Angle the pins downward, as flat as possible.

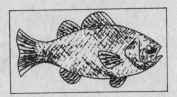

- Spray fish with hair spray to seal pores; let dry.

- Brush ink over entire fish. With clean brush, remove any little pools of ink collecting around fins or eyes.

- Lay rice paper carefully on fish; use finger tips to press paper lightly but firmly against fish.

- Slowly lift paper, peeling it off fish from one end to the other. Set print aside to dry. Re-ink fish to make a second print.

- When print is dry, you can mount it on cardboard and frame it.

NOTE: You can use dried leaves to make prints, too. Brush ink on pressed, dried leaves; arrange leaves in a pleasing group on a pad of newspapers, inked side up. Lay rice paper carefully over leaves and press with fingertips as above.

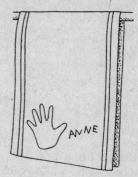

TOWEL FOR GRANDMA

Hem a length of toweling; then trace an outline of your hand on one end. Print your name beside it. Embroider hand outline and name with thread to match stripe on towel (or have Mother finish embroidery).

STOCKING SURPRISES

Crack English walnuts so that the two halves of the shells come apart. Take out the nutmeats. Put a small gift in each shell—a thimble in Mother's, a shiny penny in Daddy's, a ring in Sister's. Glue the two halves of each shell together. Paint the nuts with gold paint. Tie a ribbon with a card on it to each nut.

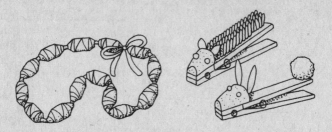

Beads: From left-over wallpaper, cut slender triangles—5 inches long, and an inch wide at the base. Beginning at the thick end of the triangle, roll it tightly around a thick broom-straw. When the bead is rolled, glue the tip of the triangle to the rolled bead. Paint with clear nail polish. Slip it off the straw. String 12 of these beads as a necklace.

Animal Clips keep papers sorted on Dad's desk, or hold Mother's recipes. To make, glue half a small cork to snapper clothespin and paint. Add eyes of map pins, ears cut from stiff paper, bristle whiskers and a cotton tail for rabbit, or a yarn mane and rubber band harness for horse.

PETS FROM PAPER BOXES

You can make animal gifts from small empty boxes of all kinds.

Porky Pig's head (thumbtack box) and matchbox legs are thumbtacked to his body. Use map pins for eyes, and glue on cork nose, paper ears and curly tail.

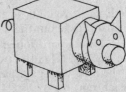

Danny Dachshund's funny body is the cardboard tube from a roll of waxed paper. Cut a cardboard circle for his head and bend sides back for ears. Cut back legs of cardboard and glue them on. Cut front legs longer than back ones; bend them back and fasten head to them with thumbtack eyes. Cut a corrugated cardboard nose and glue it to his head.

Ellie Elephant's big ears and trunk are paper. Thumbtack together the card-box body and matchbox legs. What other animals can you make? Try a dragon or a turtle.

DECORATIONS FOR HOUSE AND TREE

A Christmas Wreath: Ask Daddy to help you untwist the top of a wire coat hanger. Bend the wire into a circle. Thread Christmas tree balls on it. Tie a piece of greenery in the loop of each ball, to help hold the balls in place and to hide spots where the coat hanger shows. Fasten the ends of the coat hanger back together. Hang on door.

Door Bells: For each bell, cover a paper cup with aluminum foil. Tie a small Christmas ball to a ribbon; punch a hole in the cup; run the ribbon through.

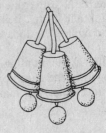

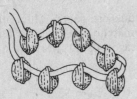

Tree Chain: Get a long ribbon. With liquid cement, glue empty walnut shells together with ribbon between them. Paint shells with enamel or nail polish. Hang chain on the Christmas tree.

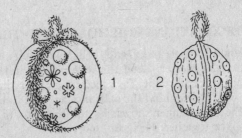

Ornaments:
1. Paint an empty moth-cake box (or other round box) with gold paint. Glue on a silver and red tinsel bow. Glue gold and red sequins and ornaments inside.

2. Glue empty walnut shell together with tinsel hanger between halves. Paint gold. Decorate with red sequins and gold glitter.

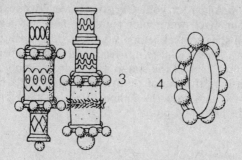

3. Paint three empty wooden spools with gold paint. Glue on gold braid and ornaments for decoration. Thread spools on a wire, with a gold ornament at each end.

4. Take the cardboard center from a roll of ribbon; paint it gold. String silver and purple ornaments on a wire; fasten wire around outside of the roll.

Dish Tree: Put modeling clay in a low dish. Stick a pine branch in it. Decorate your "tree" with small ornaments— you can cut them from colored paper or foil.

A Lemon Angel for your Christmas tree. Mix soap powder with your black watercolor paint, to make a thick mixture that will stick to slick lemon skin. Use this to paint an angel face on a lemon. Cut wings from stiff white paper and pin them to the back of the lemon. Cut a circle from gold paper, and pin it to the top of the lemon by sticking a bobby pin through it and into the lemon. Tie a loop of green yarn through the bobby pin.

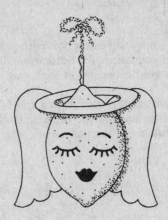

Deck the Halls & Walls

Decorating the house and filling empty spaces with the color and texture of Christmas makes every room festive. No matter that your walls are peach-colored and your rug is aubergine—the red and green stockings and the Crocheted Christmas Table Tree will go with any color scheme.

Bright colors give us a relief from the monotony of a cold and dreary winter. And warm lights satisfy a need to get away from the grayness of everyday life. As the shortest day of the year approaches, our impulses lead us to the excitement that renewal can bring. Deep within our nature the desire for change stirs. We all want to know that whatever is mundane and uneventful *can* be transformed into generous joy.

There is nothing more "natural" than placing wreaths in windows and pine boughs throughout the house. Banisters and stair railings are strung with green garlands. And centerpieces are made out of pinecones and nuts. Holly is branched on the front door and mistletoe is hung inside for all to take advantage of.

When we deck the halls and walls, we bring a feeling of merriment into a wintry world. This year think about making Christmas decorations that will give your house a charming, old-fashioned look. The Christmas stocking is especially fun to make and fun to fill. Think about how it will look brimming over with trinket boxes, apple-cheeked dolls, little wooden trucks and cars, walnuts and peppermint canes.

CHRISTMAS CAROL LIGHTS

If you have a piano, this is the perfect decoration to hang over it.

Materials
Page of music (see qualifications below)
Untempered masonite or ¼" plywood 24 × 36" (or size dictated by your music)
Rubber cement
Wood for frame, ¾ × 1½", about 10'
White glue
Skotch cleats
1" nails
1" black tape
Miniature tree lights

- Look for a favorite carol with melody notes separate from piano score. Cut away piano score; rubber cement the title, melody notes and words to white cardboard, using care to line up music staffs and verses accurately.

- Allow a generous margin around the printed material and order a negative photostat blowup from a photo copying firm, the width you want the finished picture to be, including the margins, plus an extra inch all around to wrap around the frame. Our "Silent Night" is 36 × 24″ overall, with 3″ margins at sides and top, 4½″ at bottom.

- Cut masonite or plywood to dimensions of picture and make a simple butt-joint frame to brace it on the back. Nail picture board to frame and countersink nails; edge of board should be flush with edge of frame.

- Use rubber cement to mount photostat on face of board, following this procedure carefully to get a wrinkle-free surface. Lay photostat over board and mark each corner with a pinprick. Turn photostat over and draw outline of picture on back by connecting pinmarks. Coat this area evenly with rubber cement; also coat entire surface of board with rubber cement. Let dry.

- Lay two large sheets of tracing paper over the dried cement on the photostat, leaving about 2″ uncovered down the middle. Hold the framed board over the photostat, lining up corners with the pencil outline; then press to bond the center strip (cemented surfaces will bond tightly when they touch).

- Turn over *both* board and photostat, so photostat is now on top. One side at a time, start pulling out the tracing paper—slowly—smoothing the photostat to the board as you go. Protect surface from fingermarks by rubbing with cloth.

- Cement photostat to sides of frame, too, cutting corners at a 90° angle. Cover sides of frame with black tape.

- Drill holes through notes to fit miniature light sockets. Pull lights out of sockets; push sockets into holes from back; insert lights through holes from the front. If you have more lights than notes, wind the extras through an arrangement of greens under the picture.

ADVENT CALENDAR

An Advent calendar for your door—an inside door, as it won't withstand the weather—is made with Christmas cards. It's fascinating to do, and when it's finished it will add to the air of expectancy that prevails all during December.

Use brightly colored construction paper—mine is a rosy-red—6 inches wide and 32 inches long. This means that you will have to use two pieces, each 6 inches by 16 inches, and join them at the back with cellophane tape, covering the joint on the front with garlands of holly cut from Christmas cards.

First, measure and mark the twenty-four windows and doors (one for each day of December, from the first to Christmas Eve). I made windows above the center garland and doors below it, all of them 1 inch wide except the top three.

The window at the top is 1 inch high and 2 inches wide. The two under it are 1 inch by 1½ inches. Then the next three rows of windows are 1 inch by 1 inch each. The windows just above the holly garland are 1 inch by 1½ inches.

The doors in the first row under the garland are 2 inches high, the others 2½ inches high.

When the doors and windows are all drawn with pencil, place the calendar on a board or a heavy cardboard and cut —carefully—with a razor blade across the top and bottom, and down through the middle of each window and door. Cut against a ruler edge. Bend back the shutters and doors.

Paste a strip of shelf paper on the back of the calendar, putting paste around the edges only.

Then comes the search for tiny figures to fill each door and window! Cut out little angels, kittens, and candles, and paste

them inside the shutters onto the shelf paper underneath.

On the outside of the shutters and doors paste strips of patterns in gold, or stained-glass strips from church scenes, matching and mixing as you like. You may even be lucky and find a window in your cards like the one in the center of the bottom row on mine.

The house must have a roof, of course—you'll find one somewhere among your cards. And the star of Bethlehem shines in the sky. At the bottom is the Christmas tree, set up for Christmas Eve.

Taper the top and round off the bottom, and finish off the calendar with a garland of holly like the one in the center. Open a window a day and watch the weeks go by, until it's time for Christmas.

The close-up of the Advent calendar shows the tiny figures inside the little doors—an angel singing, a little child with a muff sitting on a sled—and the patterns on the shutters. Formal Christmas cards are often edged with designs in gold and silver that can be used for this purpose.

JINGLE TREE CHRISTMAS DECORATION

designed by Mary Thomas

Ten small wreaths are joined to form this very joyful and festive decoration. Or perhaps you may wish to make only one wreath and use it for a tree ornament, package decoration, or as a lapel pin.

Size
Approx 12" wide × 15" long

Materials
Worsted weight yarn:
  1½ oz forest green

5 yds bright red
Size G aluminum crochet hook *(or size required for gauge)*
Ten 2" diameter metal macrame rings or 1¾" plastic rings
  (from sealed caps on plastic gallon milk containers)
One 1" diameter plastic ring *(for top ring)*
Ten 13 mm diameter gold jingle bells

(MATERIALS NOTE: Yarn amount needed to make one wreath is 7 yds green and ½ yd red.)

Gauge
One wreath = 3" diameter

Instructions
WREATH (make 10): With green *(leave approx 8" end for attaching jingle bell later),* make a slip knot on hook.

Rnd 1: Work 30 sc over larger size ring, join with a sl st in beg sc.

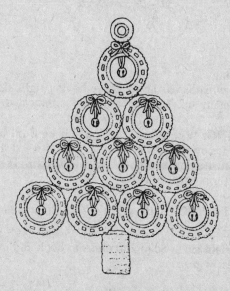

Rnd 2: * Ch 3, sl st in next sc; rep from * around, ch 3, join with a sl st in joining sl st of prev rnd. Finish off.

Slip jingle bell onto 8″ end *(left at beg of wreath)* and position at center of wreath. Tie yarn into a knot at top of bell; then weave yarn end into wreath, directly above bell *(you should now have a double strand holding bell)*.

For bow, thread 18″ length of red into tapestry or yarn needle. With right side of sts on wreath facing you, beg in ch-3 sp directly above bell and weave yarn through ch-3 sps around wreath. Tie ends into a small bow and trim.

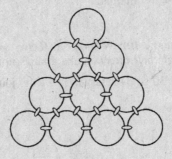

Assembling
Position wreaths as shown above having right side of each wreath facing up. Tack wreaths tog as indicated.

TOP RING: With green, make a slip knot on hook, then work 16 scs over 1″ diameter ring, join with a sl st in beg sc. Finish off, leaving approx 6″ sewing length. Tack ring securely to top wreath of tree.

TREE TRUNK: With green *(leave approx 12″ sewing length)*, ch 7.

Row 1 (right side): Sc in 2nd ch from hook and in each rem ch across = 6 sc.

Row 2: Ch 1, turn; sc in each sc across.
Rows 3 through 9: Rep Row 2, 7 times. At end of Row 9, finish off and weave in this end. Tack each end of foundation chain edge to center two bottom wreaths of tree.

CROCHETED MARY JANE CHRISTMAS SOCK

designed by Carol Wilson Mansfield and Mary Thomas

Delight a little girl on Christmas morning with this charming Mary Jane shoe complete with white sock decorated with red and green ruffles. It's cute enough to hang on her wall all year. Made in easy single crochet.

Size
Approx 6¼" wide *(across top of cuff)* × 9" long *(from folded edge of cuff to base of heel)*

Materials

Worsted weight yarn:

    2½ oz white
    ½ oz black
    8 yds red
    8 yds light green

Size H aluminum crochet hook *(or size required for gauge)*
White button *(⅝ diameter)*

Gauge

In sc, 11 sts = 3"; 4 rows = 1"

Instructions

Beg at top, with white, ch 45.

Row 1 (right side): Sc in 2nd ch from hook and in each rem ch across = 44 sc.

Rows 2 through 12: Work 11 rows even. *(NOTE: To "work even" on each row, ch 1, turn; sc in each sc across.)*

Row 13: Ch 1, turn; sc in each of first 11 sc, * dec over next 2 sc. **(To make dec: Draw up a lp in each of next 2 sc, YO hook and draw through all 3 lps on hook = dec made);** sc in each of next 9 sc; rep from * twice more = 41 sc.

Rows 14 through 18: Work 5 rows even.

Row 19: Ch 1, turn; sc in each of first 10 sc, dec over next 2 sc; sc in each of next 17 sc, dec over next 2 sc; sc in each of rem 10 sc = 39 sc.

Rows 20 through 24: Work 5 rows even.

Row 25: Ch 1, turn; sc in each of first 9 sc, * dec over next 2 sc, sc in each of next 8 sc; rep from * twice more = 36 sc.

Rows 26 through 30: Work 5 rows even. At end of Row 30, finish off white, leaving approx 24" sewing length for sewing back seam later.

INSTEP: Hold work with last row just worked at top and 24" sewing length at upper right-hand corner.

Row 1: Sk first 6 sc, join white with a sl st in next sc; ch 1, sc in each of next 23 sc (leave rem 6 sc unworked).

70

Row 2: Ch 1, turn; sk first sc, sc in each rem sc across = 22 sc.

Rows 3 through 10: Rep Row 2, 8 times. *(NOTE: You will be decreasing one sc in each row—at end of Row 9, you should have 14 sc.)* Finish off white; join black.

Rows 11 and 12: With black, work 2 rows even.

Rows 13 through 16: Rep Row 2, 4 times. *(NOTE: At end of Row 16, you should have 10 sc.)* Finish off black.

FOOT: Hold work with instep just worked at top and 24″ white sewing length at right-hand edge. Join black (leave approx 12″ end for sewing heel seam later) with a sl st in first sc at right-hand edge (next to 24″ sewing length).

Row 1: Ch 1, sc in same st as joining; 2 sc in next sc, sc in each of next 4 sc, 2 sc in next sc at inside corner. **Continuing across right edge of instep,** 2 sc in first row, sc in each of next 9 white rows, sc in each of next 5 black rows (leave last black row unworked). **Continuing across toe edge,** dec over first 2 sc, sc in each of next 6 sc, dec over last 2 sc. **Continuing across left edge of instep,** sc in each of next 5 black rows, sc in each of next 9 white rows; 2 sc in next row and in next sc at inside corner. Sc in each of next 4 sc, 2 sc in next sc, sc in last sc = 58 sc.

Row 2: Ch 1, turn; sc in each sc across.

Row 3: Ch 1, turn; sc in each of first 25 sc, dec over next 2 sc, sc in each of next 4 sc, dec over next 2 sc; sc in each of rem 25 sc = 56 sc.

Row 4: Rep Row 2.

Row 5: Ch 1, turn; sc in each of first 25 sc, (dec over next 2 sc) 3 times; sc in each of rem 25 sc = 53 sc.

Row 6: Rep Row 2.

Row 7: Ch 1, turn; sc in first sc, dec over next 2 sc, sc in each of next 23 sc; dec over next 2 sc, sc in each of next 22 sc; dec over next 2 sc, sc in last sc = 50 sc.

Row 8: Ch 1, turn; sc in each of first 23 sc, (dec over next 2 sc) twice; sc in each of rem 23 sc = 48 sc. Finish off black, leaving approx 18″ sewing length.

Finishing

With matching yarn and overcast st, sew bottom, heel and back seam.

STRAP: With black (leave approx 6" end for sewing strap to stocking later), ch 3.

Row 1: Sc in 2nd ch from hook and in next ch = 2 sc.
Row 2: Ch 1, turn; sc in each sc across.

Rep Row 2 until strap measures approx 7" long. Finish off, leaving approx 6" sewing length. Sew each end of strap to top edge of shoe (on each side of ankle), having one end of strap overlapping approx ½" of shoe. Sew button to overlapped end of strap.

CUFF: Working on inside of stocking, join white with a sl st at top edge at seam.

Rnd 1: Ch 15 (for loop), sl st in same sp as joining; sc in each of 44 sts around. *(NOTE: Do not join; work continuous rnds. Use a small safety pin or piece of yarn in contrasting color and mark first st of rnd; move marker at beg of each rnd.)*
Rnd 2: Hold loop down in front of work, * 2 sc in next sc, sc in each of next 10 sc; rep from * 3 times more = 48 sc.
Rnds 3 through 5: Work 3 rnds even. *(NOTE: To "work even," sc in each sc around for specified number of rnds, without increasing or decreasing.)* At end of Rnd 5, drop white (do not cut—will be used again later); join red (for ruffle).
Rnd 6 (ruffle): With red, * sl st **in front lp** (lp toward you—back lp will be used in next rnd) of next sc, ch 3; rep from * around. Finish off red.
Rnd 7: With white, sc **in unused lp** (back lp) of each sc around (behind ruffle) = 48 sc.
Rnd 8: Sc **in both lps** of each sc around. Finish off white; join green (for ruffle).
Rnd 9: With green, * sl st **in both lps** of next sc, ch 3; rep from * around, join with a sl st in first ch of beg ch-3. Finish off; weave in all ends. Fold down cuff.

KNITTED FISHERMAN CHRISTMAS STOCKING

designed by Mary Thomas

This beautiful heirloom stocking is knitted in the traditional off-white yarn, with interesting dimensional stitches. It may look complex, but it is really a pleasure to knit.

Size

Approx 6" wide *(across top)* × 13" long *(from folded edge of cuff to base of heel)*

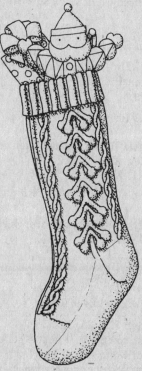

Materials

Worsted weight yarn:
  4½ oz off white

Size 8, 10" straight knitting needles *(or size required for gauge)*

Size 8, 7" double pointed needles *(abbreviated dpn)*—or size required for gauge

Size 9, 10" straight knitting needles *(for cuff only)*

Cable needle

Gauge

With smaller size needles, in stock st, 9 sts = 2"; 6 rows = 1"

Fisherman Pattern Stitches

LEFT BEADED RIB: (worked over 4 end sts)
Row 1 (wrong side): P2, K2.
Row 2: P2, K1, P1.

Rep Rows 1 and 2 for patt.

CENTER BEADED RIB: (worked over center 7 sts)
Row 1 (wrong side): K2, P3, K2.
Row 2: P2; K1, P1, K1; P2.

Rep Rows 1 and 2 for patt.

RIGHT BEADED RIB: (worked over 4 end sts)
Row 1 (wrong side): K2, P2.
Row 2: P1, K1, P2.

Rep Rows 1 and 2 for patt.

COIN CABLE: (worked over 9 sts)

Row 1 (wrong side): K2, P5, K2.
Row 2 (cable twist row): P2; sl next 4 sts onto cable needle and hold at **back** of work, K1; sl 3 sts from cable needle back onto left-hand needle (one st now on cable needle); bring

cable needle to **front** of work (between knitting needles, keeping yarn to your right) and hold at **front** of work; K3, then K1 from cable needle; P2.

Rows 3 and 5: Rep Row 1.
Rows 4 and 6: P2, K5, P2.

Rep Rows 1 through 6 for patt.

NOSEGAY: (worked over 16 sts)

Row 1 (wrong side): K7, P2, K7.
Row 2: P6, work BKC (back knit cross) (**To work BKC: Sl next st onto cable needle and hold at back of work; K1, then K1 from cable needle = BKC made**). Work FKC (front knit cross) (**To work FKC: Sl next st onto cable needle and hold at front of work; K1, then K1 from cable needle = FKC made**); P6.
Row 3: K5; work FC (front cross) (**To work FC: Sl next st onto cable needle and hold at front of work; P1, then K1 from cable needle = FC made**). P2; work BC (back cross) (**To work BC: Sl next st onto cable needle and hold at back of work; K1, then P1 from cable needle = BC made**); K5.
Row 4: P4, BC; BKC; FKC; FC, P4.
Row 5: K3, FC; K1, P4, K1; BC, K3.
Row 6: P2, BC, P1; BC, K2, FC; P1, FC, P2.
Row 7: (K2, P1) twice; K1, P2, K1; (P1, K2) twice.
Row 8: P2; work a bobble in next st [**To work bobble: Work K1, P1) twice in next st; turn, P4; turn, K4; turn, (P2 tog) twice; turn, K2 tog = bobble made**). P1, BC; P1, K2, P1; FC, P1; work a bobble in next st, P2.
Row 9: K4, P1; K2, P2, K2; P1, K4.
Row 10: P4, work a bobble in next st; P2, K2, P2; work a bobble in next st, P4.

Rep Rows 1 through 10 for patt.

Instructions

Beg at cuff, with larger size straight needles, cast on 71 sts. Work in twisted rib patt as follows:

75

Row 1 (right side): Knit **in back lp** *(Fig 1)* of first st; * P1, knit **in back lp** of next st; rep from * across.

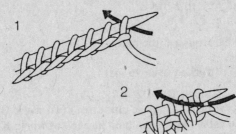

Row 2: Purl **in back lp** *(Fig 2)* of first st; * K1, purl **in back lp** of next st; rep from * across. Rep Rows 1 and 2 until cuff measures approx 1¾" from cast-on edge. Change to smaller size straight needles and continue in twisted rib patt until cuff measures approx 4" from cast-on edge, ending by working Row 1.

Next row (inc row): Continuing in twisted rib patt (Row 2), * work 5 sts, knit in front and back of next st (inc made); work 3 sts, inc; rep from * once more; work 7 sts, inc; work one st, inc; work 11 sts, inc; work one st, inc; work 7 sts, (inc, work 3 sts; inc, work 5 sts) twice = 83 sts. Now establish Fisherman Patt Sts.

Row 1 (wrong side of stocking—right side of cuff): Work Row 1 of each Patt St in the following sequence: Left Beaded Rib (4 sts); Coin Cable (9 sts); Nosegay (16 sts); Coin Cable (9 sts); Center Beaded Rib (7 sts); Coin Cable (9 sts); Nosegay (16 sts); Coin Cable (9 sts); Right Beaded Rib (4 sts).

Work even in patterns as established until 40 rows of Fisherman Patt Sts have been completed. *(NOTE: You should now have a total of 4 repeats of Nosegay Patt.)*

Dec row (wrong side): Keeping patterns as established, work

4 sts, K2 tog; work 30 sts, K2 tog; work 7 sts, K2 tog; work 30 sts, K2 tog; work 4 rem sts = 79 sts.

Keeping continuity of patterns, work even for 9 more rows. *(NOTE: You should now have a total of 50 rows of Fisherman Patt Sts—5 repeats of Nosegay Patt.)*
Dec row (wrong side): Keeping patterns as established, work 3 sts, K2 tog; work 30 sts, K2 tog; work 5 sts, K2 tog; work 30 sts, K2 tog; work 3 rem sts = 75 sts.

Keeping continuity of patterns, work even for 9 more rows. *(NOTE: You should now have a total of 60 rows of Fisherman Patt Sts—6 repeats of Nosegay Patt.)*
Dec row (wrong side): P2, K2 tog; P5, K2 tog; K6, (K2 tog) twice; K8, P5; K2, P3, K2; P5, K8; (K2 tog) twice, K6; K2 tog, P5; K2 tog, P2 = 67 sts.
Next row (right side): P1, K1, P1; twist cable over next 5 sts, P 17; twist cable over next 5 sts, work next 7 sts in Center Beaded Rib Patt as established; twist cable over next 5 sts, P 17; twist cable over next 5 sts, P1, K1, P1.
Dividing row (wrong side): With dpn, sl first st as to purl, P 15 (16 sts now on one dpn for half of heel). With straight needle, K9, work next 17 sts in patterns as established (Coin Cable—5 sts; Center Beaded Rib—7 sts; Coin Cable—5 sts); K9 (35 sts now on straight needle for instep). Sl rem 16 sts to 2nd dpn (for other half of heel).

INSTEP: Leaving 16 heel sts on each end on dpns (to be worked later), continue with smaller size straight needles and work instep on center 35 sts.

Row 1 (right side): K1, P8; work next 17 sts in patterns as established; P8, K1.
Row 2: K9, work next 17 sts in patterns as established, K9.
Rep last 2 rows until instep measures approx 5″ long, ending by twisting cables on a right-side row. *(NOTE: You should now have 5 more repeats of Coin Cable Patt.)*

Dec row (wrong side): K9, P1; (P2 tog) twice, K2; P3, K2, P1; (P2 tog) twice, K9 = 31 sts.

Cut yarn, leaving approx 24″ sewing length. Leave sts on needle (to be worked later for toe).

HEEL: Hold stocking with right side facing you and heel sts on 2 dpns at top (outer edges of stocking will be in the center between dpns). Join yarn at left outer edge of stocking (between dpns) and knit sts from left dpn onto right dpn = 32 sts now on one dpn. Continue **with both dpns** and work back and forth in rows as follows:

Row 1 (wrong side): Sl 1 as to purl, purl rem sts.
Row 2: Sl 1 as to purl, knit rem sts.

Rep Rows 1 and 2, 7 times more. *(NOTE: You should now have a total of 16 rows, ending by working a knit row.)* Now turn heel.

TURN HEEL: *(NOTE: Heel is turned by working short rows; when instructions say "turn," leave rem sts unworked, turn work and begin next row.)*

Row 1 (wrong side): Sl 1 as to purl, P 20; P2 tog, P1, turn.
Row 2: Sl 1 as to purl, K 11; sl 1 as to knit, K1, PSSO; K1, turn.
Row 3: Sl 1 as to purl, P 12; P2 tog, P1, turn.
Row 4: Sl 1 as to purl, K 13; sl 1 as to knit, K1, PSSO; K1, turn.
Row 5: Sl 1 as to purl, P 14; P2 tog, P1, turn.
Row 6: Sl 1 as to purl, K 15; sl 1 as to knit, K1, PSSO; K1, turn.
Row 7: Sl 1 as to purl, P 16; P2 tog, P1, turn.
Row 8: Sl 1 as to purl, K 17; sl 1 as to knit, K1, PSSO; K1, turn.
Row 9: Sl 1 as to purl, P 18; P2 tog, P1, turn.
Row 10: Sl 1 as to purl, K 19; sl 1 as to knit, K1, PSSO; K1 = 22 sts.

Cut yarn, leaving sts on needle. Now work gusset and foot.

GUSSET AND FOOT: With right side of heel just made facing you, join yarn (leave approx 24″ sewing length) and **with free dpn,** pick up 10 sts along right edge of heel; K 22 (heel sts), then pick up 10 sts along left edge of heel = 42 sts. Continue **with 2 dpns** and work back and forth in rows.

Row 1 (wrong side): Purl.
Row 2: K1; sl 1 as to knit, K1, PSSO; knit to last 3 sts, K2 tog, K1 = 40 sts. Rep Rows 1 and 2, 4 times more = 32 sts. Continuing in stock st, work even until piece measures same length as instep, ending by working a knit row. Do not cut yarn; continue with dpns and work toe in rnds.

TOE: Joining rnd: Leave 32 sts just worked **on first dpn; with 2nd dpn,** K 15 from straight needle (instep); **with 3rd dpn,** knit rem 16 sts from straight needle = 63 sts. Join and continue shaping in rnds as follows:

Rnd 1: Knit.
Rnd 2 (First needle): K1; sl 1 as to knit, K1, PSSO; knit to last 3 sts, K2 tog, K1. **2nd needle:** K1; sl 1 as to knit, K1, PSSO; knit rem sts. **3rd needle:** Knit to last 3 sts, K2 tog, K1 = 59 sts. Rep Rnds 1 and 2 until 19 sts rem. Cut yarn, leaving approx 12″ end. Thread into tapestry or yarn needle and weave through rem sts twice (removing knitting needles). Draw up tightly and fasten securely. Weave in all yarn ends. Weave seams tog. Fold down half of ribbing for cuff.

LOOP: With smaller size straight needles, cast on 3 sts.

Row 1 (right side): K1, P1, K1.
Row 2: Purl. Rep Rows 1 and 2 until piece measures approx 4″ long. Bind off, leaving approx 6″ sewing length. Fold in half, having wrong sides tog. Sew ends to top of stocking at seam.

Christmas Card Designs

If you send out a handmade card, you are very likely to get a letter back—people are impressed when you design your own cards. Do shop for envelopes first. You'll find blank cards with matching envelopes in art supply stores, ready to decorate. Or you can cut construction papers to fit standard-size envelopes from the stationery store.

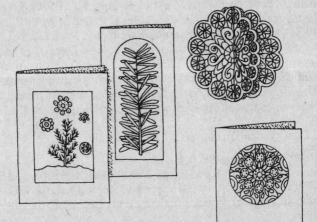

Plastic Sandwich Cards

PLASTIC SANDWICH CARDS

Materials:
Clear adhesive plastic
Leaves and evergreen sprigs (you can use either fresh or
  pressed greens)
Paper doilies
Construction paper
Rice paper

- You need two pieces of plastic for each see-through
  card. Peel backing paper from one piece, place design
  material (greens or doilies) on sticky surface; peel
  backing from second piece and lay over design. Press
  together.

- Cut out frames from construction paper and sandwich plastic designs between.

- Instead of making a see-through card, you can arrange a snow scene on colored paper (juniper sprig,
  rice-paper hill, paper-doily snowflakes) and simply
  cover it with clear plastic.

- To make hanging snowflake, sandwich two paper doilies in clear plastic. Using a long stitch on your sewing
  machine, stitch them together down the center. Write
  your name and greeting on a tag and tie to snowflake
  card.

PAPER CUTOUT CARDS

Materials
Colored construction papers
Blank cards with matching envelopes
Rubber cement
Thread

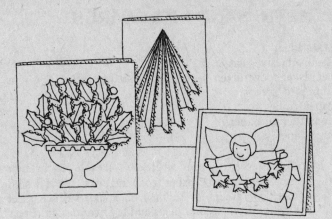

Paper Cutout Cards

- For Holly and Tree cards, cut holly leaves or tree "slivers" from colored construction paper; bend each piece down the middle by pressing paper against the edge of ruler.

- Paste the left side of each piece to card following design layout; leave right side free to bend forward slightly, giving the design a dimensional look.

- For Angel card, sketch design for flying angel with arms outstretched; trace parts onto appropriate colors of construction paper and cut out robe, head, hair, wings, hands, and feet. Glue to card with rubber cement. Cut out stars (or stick gummed stars back-to-back) and string them on a needle and thread; knot to angel's hands.

FABRIC CUTOUT CARDS

Materials
Bright printed fabrics

82

Fabric Cutout Cards

Blank cards with matching envelopes
Felt pens
Stencil paper or light-weight cardboard

- For Madonna card, cut a long, arch-shaped piece of printed fabric, plus two circles of heavy plain fabric for faces. Draw features on faces with a finepoint black felt pen. Paste faces to fabric, and fabric to card.

- For Angel and Tree cards, trace design on the front of a blank card; cut out design area with X-acto knife. Lay fabric inside card and glue front to back, sandwiching fabric between.

- Cut a stencil for Angel head and wings and use felt pens to color.

CARDS FOR CHILDREN TO MAKE

Greeting Card: Cut Christmas-tree "balls" from heavy colored paper. Punch a hole in the top and loop a string through it. Write the verse that you see below on the card ornament.

Some Christmas Cards
Are Just to See
But this one hangs
Upon Your tree
Penny

A Christmas-card Tree that is good enough to eat. Buy small peppermint sticks wrapped in cellophane. Glue each wrapped stick to a card cut from red drawing paper. Glue strips of gold paper on the card at each side of the peppermint tree, to make branches. Glue cotton "snow" at the bottom of tree. Write your greeting on the card.

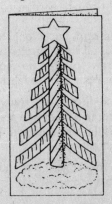

2

Holiday Foodcrafts

Planning Ahead

"Roses are things which Christmas is not a bed of them . . ."
So said Ogden Nash.

Time is something that people never have enough of and time in the Christmas season becomes precious. Everyone is busy, busy, busy working hard and playing hard. Nowadays even four-year-olds are on a tight schedule.

The nice part about the holidays is that you can drop some of your everyday activities and concentrate on the special activities of the season without feeling remiss. Put aside the book you've been hurrying to finish, tell yourself you don't *have* to get up at 6 A.M. and run those miles, and the house can wait until the very last minute to be cleaned.

The best way to organize Christmas is to decide well in advance just how much time you want to devote to holiday foodcraft. Is it one Saturday afternoon? A weekend or two? Three evenings? Then, decide what you want to make, write out a list of everything you'll need.

If you're planning to make this a family event (such as baking Christmas cookies), make sure everyone will be available. Get everything together in one place. Allow plenty of space for the project and plenty of time for cleanup. You're ready to begin!

Gifts From Your Kitchen

What could possibly make a better gift than food you have lovingly prepared? Everyone from age 1 to 101 can truly take pleasure in the joy of eating a fragrant slice of plum pudding or Panettone. Even relentless dieters delight in chewing on crunchy Pfeffernüsse cookies . . . without a thought about calories.

Holidays make us all hungry for what we know and love about Christmas past . . . the special treats that are served only at this time of the year. Use your culinary talents to make Candied Citrus Peel or Glacéed Nuts for a neighbor . . . or Pralines to delight your grandmother's sweet tooth.

Part of the fun of a gift from your kitchen is the packaging. Here's a chance to be inventive. Store-bought cookie tins can be covered with Con-Tact paper and filled with Gingerbread Cookies or Marzipan. A Christmas Twist can be wrapped in waxed paper first, and then in plain brown paper (you can cut up a paper bag) which has been decorated with a rubber stamp design. Try a rubber stamp of a unicorn. Use red stamp pad ink and stamp the unicorn on the paper, then use green ink. Overlap the unicorns, or create an allover pattern. After you've wrapped the present, tie it with a two-inch-wide red ribbon.

Pilgrim Pie can be wrapped in aluminum foil. Just add a large red-and-green-striped bow to the top. Write the recipe on an index card that you've decorated with gold stars or snowflakes. Then punch a hole in the card and string it to the package like a gift tag. You can title the recipe with your name: "Cindy's Pilgrim Pie." After all, you made it . . . and it's delicious!

A gift from your kitchen is another way to make the season more personal and less commercial. It shows you want to give something that only you can give—*your* talent, *your* energy, *your* specialty. There's nothing in the world that is more worthwhile than that. So start thinking about who would like what. Grumpy Uncle Harry? He'd probably love dozens of Meringues packed in a coffee can that's been covered with "Gnomes" paper. How about Baby Sally? A few marzipan wrapped in green cellophane and placed between the paws of a plush teddy bear would surely elicit squeals of happiness. For your favorite nephew, pack sugar cookies in a Pac-Man or Super Heroes lunch box. He can share them with his friends, or gobble them down as an after-school treat. Teenagers will love cookies titled "Late Night Snack" and packaged in a straw basket . . . or an oversized "name" coffee mug.

Whatever you decide to make and whatever packaging you decide to use, a gift from your kitchen will add irresistible sweetness to the holiday season.

SWEET DOUGH

3½ to 4½ cups all-purpose flour
⅓ cup granulated sugar
2 packages active dry yeast
1½ teaspoons salt
½ cup milk
¼ cup water
¼ cup butter or margarine
2 eggs at room temperature

In a large mixing bowl, combine 1½ cups of the flour, the sugar, undissolved yeast, and salt; mix together. In a small saucepan, heat milk, water, and butter until just warm, about 110° F. Stir into flour-sugar mixture and beat until smooth. Beat in eggs one at a time. Gradually add flour until batter becomes too stiff to mix with a spoon or beater. Turn onto a lightly floured cloth and work in enough flour to make a soft but firm dough. Knead until smooth and elastic, about 8 to 10 minutes. Place in a large greased bowl and lightly grease the top. Cover with a cloth and let rise in a warm (80° to 85° F.) place until doubled in bulk, about 1½ hours. The dough is now ready to be used in making Stollen, Panettone, Christmas Twist, or dinner rolls.

STOLLEN

½ recipe Sweet Dough
⅓ cup raisins
⅓ cup toasted slivered almonds
⅓ cup cut-up candied cherries
1½ teaspoons flour
Confectioners' sugar

Prepare the half recipe of Sweet Dough and reserve. Combine

raisins, almonds, and cherries in a bowl; add flour and toss to coat. On a lightly floured cloth, knead the almonds and fruits into the Sweet Dough until evenly distributed. Roll dough into a 7 × 12-inch oval, then fold in half lengthwise. Place on a greased baking sheet. Cover with a cloth and let rise in a warm (80° to 85° F.) place until almost double in bulk. Bake in a preheated 350° F. oven about 25 minutes, until Stollen is golden and sounds hollow when the top is tapped with the fingers. Cool on a wire rack. Sprinkle with confectioners' sugar.

PANETTONE
Christmas Bread

½ recipe Sweet Dough
2 tablespoons chopped candied orange peel
¼ cup chopped citron
¼ cup golden raisins
2 tablespoons each slivered almonds, chopped walnuts, and piñon nuts
1½ teaspoons flour
Melted butter or margarine

Prepare the half recipe of Sweet Dough and reserve. Combine candied peel, citron, raisins, and nuts in a bowl; add flour and toss to coat. On a lightly floured cloth, knead fruits and nuts into the Sweet Dough until evenly distributed. Place dough in a greased 6-inch springform pan. Cover with a cloth and let rise in a warm (80° to 85° F.) place until double in bulk. Brush top of dough with melted butter. Bake in a preheated 350° F. oven for 20 to 30 minutes, or until the bread is golden and sounds hollow when the top is tapped with the fingers.

CHRISTMAS TWIST

 ½ recipe Sweet Dough
 ½ cup golden raisins
 ½ cup chopped citron
 ½ cup cut-up candied cherries
 1 teaspoon cinnamon
 ¼ teaspoon mace
 1 teaspoon flour
 1 egg, beaten with 1 tablespoon water

Prepare the half recipe of Sweet Dough and reserve. Mix the next 6 ingredients in a bowl. On a lightly floured cloth, knead the fruit mixture into the Sweet Dough until evenly distributed. Divide dough in half and roll each half into a rope 15 inches long. Place on a greased baking sheet and twist one over the other to form a two-strand braid, pinching the ends together. Cover with a cloth and let rise in a warm (80° to 85° F.) place until almost double in bulk. Brush top and sides with egg and bake in a preheated 350° F. oven for about 20 to 30 minutes, until the twist is golden and sounds hollow when tapped with the fingers.

OLD-FASHIONED PLUM PUDDING

 ¼ cup butter or margarine
 ½ cup sugar
 1 egg
 ½ cup milk
 1 teaspoon allspice
 1 teaspoon cinnamon
 ½ teaspoon salt
 2½ cups toasted bread crumbs from firm-type bread
 1½ cups chopped apples
 1 cup chopped dates
 1 cup mixed candied fruits and peels

½ cup chopped walnuts
4 tablespoons rum
Brandy Sauce or Hard Sauce

Cream butter and sugar together. Add egg and beat well. Stir in milk and add the next 9 ingredients. Turn into a greased 1½-quart mold. Cover with a greased tightly fitting lid or with foil held in place with string. Place mold on a rack in a large deep pan. Pour in enough water to cover bottom half of the mold; cover. Simmer over low heat 4 hours, adding more water to pan as needed. Serve with Brandy Sauce or Hard Sauce. Makes 10 to 12 servings.

Hard Sauce

½ cup butter
2 cups sifted confectioners' sugar
1 tablespoon brandy, bourbon, or vanilla

Cream butter and add sugar gradually, beating until light and fluffy. Beat in flavoring. Makes 1½ cups.

Brandy Sauce

½ cup butter or margarine
2 cups sifted confectioners' sugar
2 egg yolks
½ cup heavy cream
2 tablespoons brandy or bourbon

Cream butter and sugar and beat until light. Add egg yolks and beat until thick and lemon-colored; beat in cream. Cook over simmering water for 6 minutes, stirring constantly. Add brandy or bourbon and serve warm. Makes 2½ cups.

PILGRIM PIE

1 9-inch pie shell
2 cups pumpkin, fresh or canned
¾ cup light brown sugar, firmly packed
½ teaspoon salt
1 teaspoon cinnamon
½ teaspoon each ginger and nutmeg
¼ teaspoon each ground allspice and cloves
2 eggs
1 cup heavy cream
6 tablespoons rum, cider, or applejack

Place pie shell in the refrigerator, uncooked, to chill. In a medium-sized saucepan, heat pumpkin and cook about 5 minutes to dry out, stirring to prevent burning. Stir in the sugar, salt, and the 5 spices. In a medium-sized bowl, beat the eggs until thick and lemon-colored; add cream and rum. Stir into the pumpkin mixture. Strain through a fine strainer and pour into the chilled unbaked shell. Bake in a preheated 450° F. oven for 15 minutes. If necessary, cover edges with strips of foil to keep from browning too rapidly. Reduce heat to 300° F. and bake 30 to 40 minutes more or until pie is set.

PRALINES

2 cups sugar
¾ teaspoon baking soda
1 cup light cream
1½ tablespoons butter or margarine
2 cups pecan halves

Combine sugar and soda in a 3-quart saucepan. Add cream and stir to dissolve sugar. Bring to a boil over medium heat, stirring occasionally. When mixture starts to boil, reduce heat. The mixture will gradually turn golden as it cooks. Boil until syrup forms a soft ball when a small amount is dropped into a cup of cold water, or reaches 234° F. on a candy thermometer. Remove pan from heat and add butter. Stir in pecans and beat just until thick enough to drop from a metal spoon. Drop candy on waxed paper placed on a cookie sheet. If necessary, add a tablespoon or so of hot water to keep candy at the right consistency for dropping from spoon. Cool until firm before removing. Makes about 1 dozen 2½-inch pralines.

PFEFFERNÜSSE

> 3 eggs
> 1 cup sugar
> 3 cups all-purpose flour
> ½ teaspoon baking powder
> ½ teaspoon baking soda
> ¼ teaspoon salt
> ¼ teaspoon freshly ground pepper
> ½ teaspoon ground cloves
> 1½ teaspoons cinnamon
> ¼ cup finely ground blanched almonds
> Confectioners' sugar or frosting (optional)

Beat eggs until light and thick. Gradually add sugar while continuing to beat. Sift together the next 7 ingredients and add, a little at a time, to the egg mixture. Beat in the almonds. Chill dough for 1 hour or more for easier handling. Form rounded teaspoons of dough and roll between floured palms into balls about 1¼ inches in diameter. Place on a greased cookie sheet 1 inch apart. Bake in a preheated 350° F. oven for about 12 minutes, or until lightly browned on bottom. Do not overcook, because Pfeffernüsse harden after removal from the oven. They may be rolled in sugar while warm, or frosted if desired. Store in an airtight container with a slice of apple for at least a week. Makes about 4 dozen Pfeffer-nüsse.

GLACÉED NUTS

> 2 cups granulated sugar
> ⅛ teaspoon cream of tartar
> ½ cup water
> ⅓ cup each almonds, pecan halves, and cashews

Combine sugar, cream of tartar, and water in a small heavy saucepan. Place over medium heat and stir constantly until sugar is dissolved. Wipe crystals from sides of pan. Boil, without stirring, to 240° F. on a candy thermometer, or until syrup forms a soft ball when dropped in cold water. Add nuts and continue to boil to 300° F., the hard-crack stage, when a small amount tested in cold water forms a brittle thread. Pour into a large sieve; drain. Turn onto a buttered cookie sheet and separate the nuts quickly with two forks. When cool, store in an airtight container.

Do not attempt to glacé more than 1 cup of nuts at a time unless someone is available to help separate the nuts before they harden.

CANDIED CITRUS PEEL

> 3 large oranges
> 3 large grapefruit
> 1½ cups water
> 3 cups granulated sugar
> 3 tablespoons honey
> ⅛ teaspoon salt
> 1 teaspoon unflavored gelatin

94

Cut oranges into fourths and grapefruit into eighths. Remove pulp and scrape away all the white part. Cut peel into ½-inch strips. Place peel in a 2-quart saucepan, cover with water, and simmer 15 minutes; drain and discard the water. Pour over the peel 1¼ cups of the measured water, 2 cups of the sugar, the honey, and the salt. Cook 45 minutes over low heat, stirring occasionally. Just before removing from heat, soften gelatin in remaining ¼ cup of water and add to hot mixture. Stir to dissolve. Let cool, and drain well in a colander. Roll the strips of peel in the remaining 1 cup of sugar, and let dry overnight on a baking sheet lined with waxed paper. Store in a tightly covered container. The peel will keep moist for several weeks. Makes about 12 ounces.

MERINGUES

> 6 egg whites at room temperature
> ⅛ teaspoon cream of tartar
> 1½ cups granulated sugar
> ½ teaspoon vanilla
> Candy decorations

In a large bowl with an electric mixer at high speed, beat egg whites until frothy. Add cream of tartar and continue to beat until soft peaks form. Very slowly add sugar while beating, about 12 minutes. Add vanilla and beat until meringue looks glossy and holds stiff peaks. Line a baking sheet with ungreased brown paper. Scoop meringue onto the paper, forming desired shapes with a spoon, or pipe with a pastry tube. Decorate with colored sugar crystals, spangles, or silver shot. Bake in a preheated 200° F. oven for about 2 hours or until very dry but still white. Makes about 2 dozen 2-inch meringues.

MARZIPAN

1 can (8 ounces) almond paste
2 tablespoons slightly beaten egg white
1 cup sifted confectioners' sugar

In a medium-sized bowl, break up almond paste with a fork. Add egg white and work in well. Knead in the sugar until the mixture is stiff enough to form into desired shapes.

Fruits and vegetables may be modeled from marzipan and tinted with food coloring. Marzipan may be used to stuff dried apricots, figs, and dates; or it may be rolled into candies, spread with Fondant Frosting and topped with an almond, pecan, or walnut. Makes about 1½ dozen candies 1½ × ¾ × ¾ inches, or about 36 fillings for dried fruits.

Table Decorations

After you've decked the walls and halls, you'll want to think about table decorations. On the following pages you will find designs and instructions for making attractive and unusual centerpieces that will add just the right touch to a Christmas Eve caroling party or a New Year's Day brunch. Or, if you like, they can be used in an entryway, on a coffee table, a buffet, or a mantel. Use your imagination and add pine boughs, red and green Christmas balls, and straw angels. And a bright red tablecloth will show everything off to its best advantage. Each is inexpensive, fun to make, and is a unique and interesting conversation piece. Children will especially like to help with making the Popcorn Tree or the Apple Pyramid.

Whichever one you decide on, the satisfaction of creating and using your handiwork will be enormous . . . and a treat for your family and friends. Think about how much fun it will be to decorate the table with something as charming as an epergne with Quick Miniature Fruitcakes. Picture glistening punch glasses and plates waiting invitingly for the delights to come—this is part of what Christmas is about.

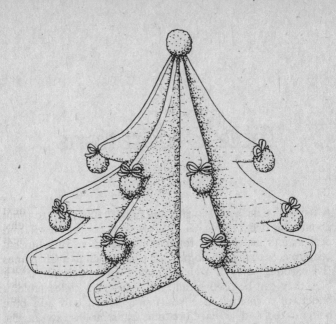

CROCHETED CHRISTMAS TABLE TREE

designed by Mary Thomas

Decorate your home for the holidays with this lovely crocheted tree ideal for a table centerpiece. If you wish, you can
use purchased pompons or small ornaments in place of yarn
pompons.

Size
Approx 13½ " tall *(including pompon on top)*

Materials
Worsted weight yarn:
   11 oz ombre in shades of green

1 oz bright red *(for pompons)*
5 yds bright yellow *(for pompon at top of tree)*
Size J aluminum crochet hook *(or size required for gauge)*
Polyester fiber *(for stuffing)*

Gauge
In sc, 13 sts = 4"; 4 rows = 1"

Instructions

(Make 6) Beg at bottom edge, with ombre, ch 57.
Row 1: Sc in 2nd ch from hook, sk next ch, sc in each of next 7 chs; hdc in each of next 5 chs, dc in each of next 28 chs; hdc in each of next 5 chs, sc in each of next 7 chs; sk next ch, sc in last ch = 54 sts.
Row 2: Ch 1, turn; sk first sc, dec over next 2 sc **[To work dec: Draw up a lp in each of next 2 sc (3 lps now on hook), YO hook and draw through all 3 lps on hook = dec made].** Sc in each rem st across to last 3 sc, sk next sc, dec over last 2 sc = 50 sc.
Row 3: Ch 1, turn; sk first sc, sc in each of next 17 sc, hdc in each of next 14 sc; sc in each of next 16 sc, sk next sc, sc in last sc = 48 sts.
Row 4: Ch 1, turn; sk first sc, sc in each rem st across to last 2 sc; sk next sc, sc in last sc = 46 sc.
Rows 5 through 12: Rep Row 4, 8 times. *(NOTE: At end of Row 12, you should have 30 sc.)*
Row 13: Ch 9 (for branch), turn; sc in 2nd ch from hook, sk next ch, sc in each of rem 6 chs; sc in each rem sc across = 37 sc.
Row 14: Ch 9 (for branch), turn; sc in 2nd ch from hook, sk next ch, sc in each of rem 6 chs; sc in each rem sc across to last 3 sc, sk next sc, dec over last 2 sc = 42 sc.
Row 15: Ch 1, turn; sk first sc, sc in each rem sc across to last 3 sc; sk next sc, dec over last 2 sc = 39 sc.
Rows 16 through 26: Rep Row 4, 11 times. *(NOTE: At end of Row 26, you should have 17 sc.)*

Row 27: Ch 9 (for branch), turn; sc in 2nd ch from hook, sk next ch, sc in each of rem 6 chs; sc in each rem sc across to last 2 sc, sk next sc, sc in last sc = 23 sc.

Row 28: Rep Row 14 = 28 sc.

Row 29: Rep Row 15 = 25 sc.

Rows 30 through 34: Rep Row 4, 5 times. *(NOTE: At end of Row 34, you should have 15 sc.)*

Row 35: Ch 1, turn; sc in each sc across.

Row 36: Rep Row 4 = 13 sc.

Rows 37 through 46: Rep Rows 35 and 36, 5 times. *(NOTE: At end of Row 46, you should have 3 sc.)*

Row 47: Ch 1, turn; sc in each sc across.

Row 48: Ch 1, turn; sk first sc, dec over last 2 sc. Finish off; weave in ends.

Assembling

Join two pieces tog to form one section of tree as follows: Hold both pieces tog with edges carefully matched. Leaving approx 7″ open at center bottom for stuffing later, beg at bottom and sc edges tog around with ombre—be sure to work through matching sts/rows around and to work 3 sc at tip

of each branch and at center top. Finish off, leaving approx 16" sewing length. Stuff tip of each branch lightly (do not overstuff). Join rem pieces tog in same manner to form other two sections of tree and lightly stuff tip of each branch. Place all 3 sections of tree just made on top of each other, having edges in same alignment. Thread approx 48" strand of ombre into a tapestry or yarn needle. Using the backstitch sewing method, beg at top and sew all 3 sections tog down the center ending at bottom edge. Finish stuffing and shaping sections, then sew bottom openings closed.

POMPONS: Make 12, 1" diameter red pompons, leaving tying ends of each pompon uncut. Using these yarn ends, attach one pompon under tip of each of the 12 upper branches around tree and tie ends into a small bow. Then make one, 1" diameter yellow pompon and attach securely to top of tree.

POPCORN TREE

> Butter or margarine
> 8 cups popped popcorn
> 1 cup sugar
> ⅓ cup light corn syrup
> ⅓ cup water
> Styrofoam cone 12 inches high with a 3½-inch base
> Wood picks
> Small gumdrops
> Green foliage (optional)

Place the popcorn in a large buttered bowl. Combine sugar, corn syrup, and water in a 1-quart saucepan. Cook over medium heat, without stirring, until syrup reaches 240° F. on a candy thermometer, or forms a soft ball when a small amount is dropped into a cup of cold water. Pour hot syrup over popcorn. Immediately mix and toss the popcorn

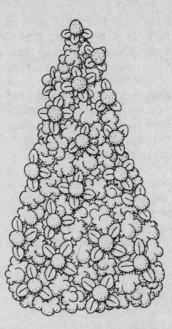

with two forks until well coated. Working rapidly, pull off small amounts and form into balls of graduated sizes, placing them on waxed paper. When ready to assemble, place a pick in each ball and stick into the Styrofoam cone to form the tree, using smaller balls for the top. Place gumdrops on picks and insert to resemble ornaments. Decorate with green foliage if desired.

Popcorn may also be made into 12 popcorn balls or 3 balls of graduated size to form a snowman.

APPLE PYRAMID

The traditional apple pyramid, sometimes called the Hospitality Pyramid, comes to us from England. It was a popular Christmas centerpiece during the eighteenth and nineteenth

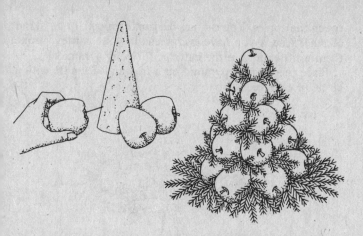

centuries. It can be used on the Christmas dinner table, on a mantel, or on a hall table. The fragrance of apples and evergreens signifies the season, giving an extra dimension to the treelike form. It is easy to make and will last for more than a week.

Start with a Styrofoam cone about 10 inches tall, thirteen regular-size apples, and about ten small apples. You will also need about 5 feet of ordinary iron wire of 14 gauge, and several sprays of evergreens. Shine up the apples before you begin the project.

In the bottom row of the pyramid there are seven apples. To attach the apples to the cone, cut seven pieces of wire, each about 4 inches long. Impale an apple on one end of each wire and insert the other end in the cone. Try to space the apples evenly, and remember that the spaces in between will be filled with evergreens. The second row from the bottom will take six apples. For the next three rows, use the smaller apples—five for the third row, four for the fourth, and one nice one for the very top of the cone. As the cone becomes narrower, shorten your pieces of wire.

When all the apples are in place, insert short sprigs of evergreens into the Styrofoam cone to fill in the spaces between the apples. You can use balsam, hemlock, or any kind of pine. And if you have evergreens in your garden, prune them a little and use the cuttings for your pyramid.

Place the finished pyramid on a tray and decorate with a circle of evergreens.

QUICK MINIATURE FRUITCAKES

24 miniature-sized fluted foil baking cups
1 pound or 2 cups mixed chopped candied fruits
¾ cup golden raisins
1 cup broken walnuts
1½ cups sifted all-purpose flour
1 teaspoon double-acting baking powder
¼ teaspoon salt

¼ teaspoon each (ground) nutmeg, clove, allspice, cinnamon, ginger
½ cup sugar
½ cup cooking oil
2 eggs, unbeaten
3 tablespoons sherry or orange juice
Candied cherries (optional)

Remove paper liners from foil cups and place cups on a
baking sheet. Put candied fruits, raisins, and walnuts in a
bowl. Add flour, baking powder, salt, and spices. Toss
thoroughly to coat all fruits and nuts. Add sugar, oil, eggs,
and sherry or orange juice, and stir to blend well. Spoon into
the foil cups. Bake in a preheated 275° F. oven for 1 hour.
If desired, decorate the cakes with candied cherries. Store in
an airtight container. Makes 24 cakes.

Old-Fashioned
Cookie Ornaments

Bright and sugary cookies make a Christmas tree look really charming and old-fashioned. You can decorate the whole tree with just cookie hearts, bells, angels, and gingerbread men, all strung with red satiny ribbons . . . or you can hang the cookies alongside gold and silver ornaments or jingle tree Christmas decorations.

Children love making holiday cookies. It is always a special treat to see their eager faces when the cookie cutters are brought out. And it's a pleasure to see how much enjoyment they get out of shaping the little Santas and trees. As the sweet smell of baking fills the house and the windows steam and frost, take time out to read your favorite Christmas story aloud. What child can resist the fairytale of a toy that comes to life? Or the story of The Little Drummer Boy?

After all the cookies are decorated, it's time to taste a few. Then, one by one, find a place on the tree for each extra-special star and angel.

The mouth-watering cookies can also be a feast to the eye if you arrange them on a wooden "shelf-tree" (see illustration p. 108) or a small garden trellis. The delightful shapes will give your mantel or buffet a festive look that nourishes the spirit and captures the feeling of a bygone day.

LET'S BEGIN—A FEW TIPS

1 Rolling cookie dough isn't hard if you chill the dough first and use a pastry cloth and stockinet-covered rolling pin. Rub a little flour into the pastry cloth with your hand. It will disappear into the meshes in the cloth. Roll the stockinet-covered rolling pin around on the floured cloth. When you roll out chilled cookie dough, it will not stick either to cloth or pin. What's more important, the dough will not take up extra flour, which would make your cookies tough.

2 How to Flour Cookie Cutter: Spoon a little flour into a small bowl. Dip the cookie cutter into the flour and tap it gently on the edge of the bowl to shake off the loose flour. Flouring keeps the rolled cookie dough from sticking to the cutter. Flour it as many times as you need to while cutting out cookies.

3 Cookies for the Christmas Tree: Cut paper drinking straws into 1″ lengths. Push one into each unbaked cookie on baking sheet. Bake cookies and remove straws by gently twisting them out while cookies are still hot. Frost cooled cookies and decorate with little candies, or as you like. Pull narrow, bright-colored ribbons through cookies and tie them on the Christmas tree.

SUGAR COOKIES

1½ cups sugar
1 cup shortening
2 eggs, well beaten
1½ teaspoons vanilla
3½ cups sifted all-purpose flour
1 teaspoon baking powder

½ teaspoon salt
Tinted frosting, Fondant Frosting, raisins, colored sugar
   (optional)

Cream sugar and shortening until light and fluffy; beat in
eggs and vanilla. Sift in flour, baking powder, and salt; blend
well. Pat into a ball, wrap in foil, and chill until firm. Divide
the dough into fourths; work with one fourth at a time,
refrigerating the remainder. Roll out to desired thickness for
various sizes and shapes of cookies. Place on a greased cookie
sheet and bake in a preheated 375° F. oven until the edges are
golden, about 5 to 7 minutes. Cool slightly before removing
to a wire rack.

Decorate as desired with tinted frosting, raisins, or colored
sugar. Dough may be cut with cookie cutters or with a knife
from cardboard patterns. Picture cutouts may be "pasted" on
with Fondant Frosting. Makes about 4 dozen cookies.

Fondant Frosting

2 cups sifted confectioners' sugar
1½ teaspoons lemon juice or vanilla
2 to 3 tablespoons water

In a medium-sized bowl, mix sugar, lemon juice, and enough
water for desired consistency. Stir until smooth. Store the
Fondant Frosting in a covered jar in refrigerator. Remove
one hour before using to soften. Spread over slightly warm
breads, or use for decorating or frosting cookies. Makes
about ¾ cup.

GINGERBREAD COOKIES

⅓ cup brown sugar, firmly packed
⅓ cup butter, margarine, or shortening
⅔ cup molasses
1 egg, unbeaten
3 cups sifted all-purpose flour
1 tablespoon baking powder
1½ teaspoons ground ginger
½ teaspoon salt

Cream sugar and shortening until light and fluffy. Beat in molasses and egg. Sift in flour, baking powder, ginger, and salt; blend well. Chill 2 or more hours until firm enough to roll. Divide dough into fourths; work with one fourth at a time, refrigerating the remainder. Roll out to desired thickness for various sizes and shapes of cookies. Place on a greased cookie sheet and bake in a preheated 350° F. oven until firm, about 5 to 7 minutes. Cool slightly before removing to a wire rack. Makes about 2 dozen 4- to 6-inch cookies.

CHOCOLATE SUGAR COOKIES

Frost with confectioners' sugar icing.

¾ cup shortening
1 cup sugar
1 egg
¼ cup light corn syrup
2 squares unsweetened chocolate, melted
2 cups flour
1 teaspoon baking soda
¼ teaspoon salt
1 teaspoon ground cinnamon

• Beat shortening and sugar together until light and

110

fluffy. Add egg and beat to mix well. Stir in syrup and melted chocolate.

- Stir flour in canister or bag to loosen it, and spoon it lightly into flour-measuring cup until it overflows. Level the top by sweeping across it with the straight edge of a knife. Sift measured flour with baking soda, salt, and cinnamon. Stir into sugar-shortening mixture. Divide dough in half and chill in refrigerator 1 hour or until dough is easy to handle.

- Start heating oven to 350°. Roll dough, half of it at a time, until it is ⅛ inch thick. Cut with Christmas cookie cutters.

- Use a wide spatula to place cookies ½ inch apart on ungreased baking sheet.

- Bake 10 to 12 minutes, or until cookies are lightly browned at edges.

- Remove baking sheet from oven at once; use a wide spatula to place cookies on wire cooling rack. Makes about 24 cookies.

Pomanders

Remember when you used to make pomanders in kindergarten, and how pleased your mother was when she hung them in the front closet?

Oranges or lemons can be stuck all over with whole cloves and then left in a dry place for about three weeks. Tie a

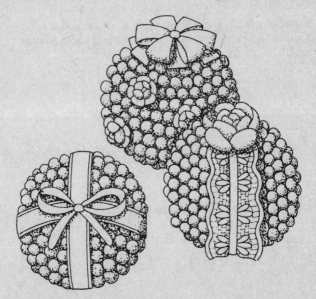

ribbon around the pomander and decorate it with straw flowers, lace, beads, or gold-foil hearts.

Children love sticking the cloves into oranges and lemons —the activity seems to fascinate them. And even the smallest ones enjoy making precise little paths in the thick-skinned fruits.

Cranberry & Popcorn Swags

If you want to give your Christmas tree a really traditional look, there's nothing more appealing than Cranberry & Popcorn Swags. They're easy and fun to make. Just pop the popcorn (following the directions). You'll need about four quarts of popped corn and one pound of cranberries. This should make eight yards of strands. Use a large needle and strong buttonhole thread. Each thread should be a yard long. Then thread the popcorn and cranberries in any pattern you like. Say, three popcorn kernels and then a berry, then two popcorn kernels and two berries. When you're done with that strand, tie the end of the thread to the next one, and start threading the second strand.

Cranberry & Popcorn Swags are pure enjoyment for children. They love stringing the corn and berries (and munching popcorn as they work). There's a lot of imagination involved in creating the patterns . . . and then swirling them around the tree.

Cranberry & Popcorn Swags are fun to make and perfect for a tree-trimming party. It's an easy way to bring family and friends together in a spirit of old-fashioned conviviality. And when you have hung the last strand, it's time to sing Christmas carols . . . and then have a cup of ice-cold eggnog and a thick slice of Stollen.